AND THEN THE END WILL COME

MATTHEW 24:14

And this gospel of the kingdom will be preached in the whole world as a testimony to all nations, and then the end will come.

Vision 2025

By the year 2025 a Bible IN EVERY LANGUAGE!

Wycliffe Associates

WestBow Press books may be ordered through booksellers or by contacting:

WestBow Press
A Division of Thomas Nelson & Zondervan
1663 Liberty Drive
Bloomington, IN 47403
www.westbowpress.com
1 (844) 714-3454

ISBN: 978-1-9736-9415-1 (sc)

Library of Congress Control Number: 2020911523

Print information available on the last page.

WestBow Press rev. date: 02/11/2021

WESTBOW
PRESS®
A DIVISION OF THOMAS NELSON
& ZONDERVAN

And this gospel of the kingdom will be preached in the whole world as a testimony to all nations, and then the end will come.

Vision 2025

By the year 2025 a Bible IN EVERY LANGUAGE!
Wycliffe Associates

Table of Contents

Introduction

As Jesus was sitting on the Mount of Olives, the disciples came to Him privately. "Tell us," they said "when will this happen (destruction of the temple), and what will be the sign of your coming and of the end of the age?" Matthew 24:3

Jesus then gives many signs that precedes His return and then tells of the greatest final event which is the title of this writing. He also tells them that only the Father knows at that time (Jesus did not know then, as He emptied Himself when He left Heaven) when our Savior will return. I believe the graph from Wycliffe Translators gives the most accurate time in His-story when He will return.

To really grasp the full meaning of the "line" you must now look at history from a different perspective. It is not just the happenings in the world as taught in the textbooks but the real purpose of the events. Satan knows the scriptures and must delay the "line" as he cannot stop it. Look at the graph and see how little progress was made in spreading the good news. From Adam until John Wycliffe in the 1380's the line was straight. God used other forces and it went up dramatically after year 1800 AD! Can you see the fantastic change in just 200 years? Satan sees this too and he knows Matthew 24:14. The delaying destructions he causes are in the signs our Savior has given and he is getting desperate to stop the line. He caused World War I and II to stop Christians in Europe and America from doing missions and spreading the Word. These are not just historical events but clearly a major part of the spiritual battle designed to stop the progress of the graph.

The United States is a special country purposed by God. At this time, we are commemorating the 75th year anniversary of D-Day. As mentioned in Chapter 3, I believe that those who died were injured or who served, will have special favor with God on the judgment day as they suffered and some died, for the Gospel's sake. That is true for those who were Christians and those who were not.

For Jesus to return there must be the fulness of the Jews. So Satan had in mind to destroy Gods beloved people and murdered 6 million of them in WWII. Also, the fulness of the Gentiles must occur, that is the Word throughout the entire world. The world wars plus other events were to stop that. Then it was communism. Then the liberalization of the churches. Now the attempts to destroy the US economy, which finances most of the mission work, by flooding the country with illegal immigrants, violent gangs, diseases, and drugs. Again, as times will be getting very difficult and persecution increases, the intensity of the spiritual battle is caused by the progress of the line on the graph. As Chapter 6 pleads, let all the churches unite for the final battle!

Preface

History is His Story and the driving engine (force, power) of this event is Psalm 103:11-12 and ultimately clarified in John 3:16. The longing of God's people is to see the promised Son of God, Yahweh (Messiah, Jesus Christ). Many books were written and predictions made as to the day of His return. It is the most awesome occurrence that will happen in world history in addition to his birth and creates the most excitement and interest for God's people. That makes this subject very popular and of most interest to those who will hear Jesus call his/her name at His return.

This book is not written as an end times book to set a date of Jesus return. Rather it is to challenge all churches who love Him and his appearing with a factual time structure line that can be forced to culmination. We have the "power," only being enabled by the Holy Spirit of course, to bring Him back! We should all lay aside the "adiaphorah" which can divide and cause divergence and as one body, focus on this one goal! From the graph you can see that the goal can be achieved in the lifetime of many living today. This should be an impetus to work harder and faster to fulfil His command to all of us to "go and make disciples of all nations" Matthew 28:19. This is the eleventh commandment that results from the summary to love God above all and your neighbor as yourself.

God, who comforts us with the fact that He directs our steps (Proverbs 16:9 & 19:21) moved me to begin a business which was often a difficult journey. Soon after I started such a venture I received a pamphlet from Wycliffe Bible Translators (1983) with the time line that is on the cover of this book. I became excited as this picture made clear how we, as Christians, could bring Jesus back as He had promised. We could impact His return by getting the Gospel translated into all languages as He commands us to do in Matthew 24:14 "And this gospel of the kingdom will be preached in the whole world as a testimony to all nations, and then the end will come." The time line can be moved to its end by supporting, praying for, and working with the Holy Spirit for all the ministries that appear as the Holy Spirit is being poured out. (Joel 2:28-29) The goal of the business was to finance many organizations doing this work.

The graph on the cover filled me with anticipation and direction for my life. I wanted to have a part of that historical line and put pressure on its completion with Jesus return. Finally, a sign of His return that gives the clearest picture of a "date" for which many people are looking for! This is a clear idea of the direction of History, giving meaning to world events that lead to its culmination or end.

This time line, in reality, reveals world history from the beginning to its end. It should motivate us to unite for the ultimate goal of Jesus return. It is an interpretive tool for world events and helps explain human occurrences influenced by the evil one. He is well aware he is finished when the line is complete and is trying to stop the propagation of the Gospel any way he can.

I believe a book could be written on each subject covered by each chapter of this book. However, this book by design is not large and the chapters are short, as Dr. McGee said many times, that for people to reach and understand, the "cookies must be put on the lower shelf". In other words, this is not a theological dissertation but hopefully a writing that can be easily read and understood at any age.

CHAPTER 1

Moving the Line

The Eleventh Commandment results from the summary of the law – "love God above all and your neighbor as yourself." Now this fact puts pressure on The Line and gives power to God's people to bring Jesus back. The main reason for this writing is to plead with and urge the church militant to unite. Let us not let our differences in our "adiaphora" keep us apart in this endeavor. We have the power to bring Him back! Let that fact excite us to vigorously combine our efforts to push The Line to completion. I believe there are many denominations like the Baptist, Lutherans, Presbyterians, Reformed, Christian Reformed, and many others because our God loves variety. Would you like all your children to look and act alike? The differences make us study the Scriptures to discern where and why we differ. So, though we may differ in how we meet, when we meet, how we conduct our services, or the sacraments, these are not the cause of our salvation. We know that Jesus is the only way to the Father, having been purchased by his blood and sacrifice on the cross revealed to us by the leading of the Holy Spirit. In other words, this is for the true church, the people of God to whom I appeal to "hasten" His return. The true church, the triumphant in Heaven, will not have the differences in worship, loving God, and enjoying Him forever. Let us exhibit this trust of unity in Christ, not allowing our differences to hinder our obedience to the Eleventh Commandment.

My hope is that we could create a Synod or entity that would be assigned this task and unite Gods people around the world to reach every tongue and tribe with the Gospel. Maybe our quest to build local churches in physical size and for personal satisfaction should be tempered and use more of our resources, prayers, and time to get the Good News to the entire world.

As Satan sees the time line of Christs return move to completion, he will become more violent, more desperate as his end comes closer. Expect more hardships and persecution. We already see the opposition increase as nations, including the United States, turn their backs on Him. But it is impossible to stop this work of the true church on earth.

Following is information given by Wycliffe Translators that explains events that accompanied the time line graph. Wycliffe is responsible for the graph for which I am grateful.

A deep conviction of the importance of the Bible's message is what has motivated Bible translators throughout the ages. Committed to making that message clear at any cost, Bible translators have given years, and sometimes their very lives, to see the task completed. At the time of this writing Wycliffe reported the murder of four national translators in a raid in a translation office in the Middle East and demolishing of the manuscripts.

President Reagan has proclaimed 1983 "The Year of the Bible." While making the proclamation, he said, "Inside (the Bible's) pages lie all the answers to all the problems man has ever known."

A deep conviction of the importance of the Bibles message is what has motivated Bible translators throughout the ages. Committed to making that message clear at any cost, Bible translators have given years, and sometimes their very lives, to see the task completed.

The task was begun some 200 years before Christ, when 70 scholars in Egypt translated the Hebrew Scriptures into Greek. Look at the flatness of the line until the 15th century. Very dramatic! It is still going on. In fact, the vision has never burned as brightly as it burns now. Before 1900, 523 language groups received their first piece of translated Scripture. Between 1900 and 1982 the figure was 1,240.

During the course of history Bible portions have been translated and published in 1,763 languages. More specifically:

2019	1983	
698	279	language groups have had a complete Bible.
1548	551	language groups have had a complete Testament but not the whole Bible.
1138	933	language groups have had at least one complete book but not a whole New Testament.
3384	1.763	Total

2115 languages need translation or preparatory work to begin.

*Figures courtesy of the American Bible Society 1983 and Wycliffe Translators 2019.

Who have the translations been for?

Prior to 1800: The majority of Bible translators prior to 1800 were bilingual Christians who translated from another language into their own mother tongue. Jerome, for example, translated into Latin, Wycliffe into English and Luther into German. They translated for established churches which had heard the gospel long before and had been existing on foreign language Scriptures.

After 1800: Around 1800 European Protestants began to take the Good News around the world. Their mission fields were generally colonies governed by their respective countries. The Englishman William Carey, for instance, went to the British colony of India. Increasingly, Bible translators after 1800 were missionaries who translated into languages they learned in order to preach the gospel. They used their translation for evangelism, teaching, church planting and church growth. The Bible Society movement, with its burden for Scripture distribution, coincided with this era.

After 1950: By the middle of the twentieth century, the colonial era was coming to an end. A strong worldwide movement for political independence brought many new independent nations into being. Increasingly, many of these nations are requiring that their own people take over tasks previously done by foreigners. The world wars, meant by Satan to destroy, helped interaction between those counties that had the scriptures with those who did not. In fact our troops on foreign soil helped spread the gospel.

Today there is a need for both kinds of Bible translators – those who translate into their mother tongue and those who translate into an acquired language.

Our members continue to pioneer, learning languages in order to translate, as well as encouraging others to develop the skills and vision for Bible translation. Where there are mother tongue speakers with a vision to translate, we train them in vital linguistic and translation skills and provide consultant help. We provide similar help for speakers of national languages, such as Spanish or French, who are translating for a minority group.

Who's done the translations?

Prior to 1450: During the Middle Ages there was little vision for Scriptures in a person's mother tongue. The Roman Catholic Church insisted on the use of Jerome's Latin version. It discouraged the use of Scriptures by anyone except clergy, scholars and kings, on the grounds that the unlearned would misinterpret it. Few people, even among the clergy, lawyers and kings, could read. Handwritten copies of the Bible were extremely expensive. The few translations that were produced were in the dominant languages of the ancient world, such as Latin and Coptic, and in early European languages.

Around 1450: Around 1450 the climate for bible translation changed. The Renaissance brought a new emphasis on learning, so that even the common man was encouraged to learn to read. The Reformation stressed the importance of knowing Scripture. Gutenberg's invention of a printing press with movable type brought the price of a Bible within the reach of ordinary people. As a result of all this, there was new interest in the translation of the Bible into the major languages of Europe.

1933-1934: The year 1933 was a landmark year for Bible translation. Spiritual and secular developments came together to make it the beginning of the modern Bible translation movement for ethnic people groups.

1. In Keswick, New Jersey, L.L. Legters reported to the Keswick conference on a trip to South America. The Lord sent an unusual burden on the conferees to pray for unreached tribes.
2. In Keswick, England, John Savage of Peru also challenged conferees to pray for the unreached tribes. Again the Lord sent an unusual burden.
3. In the scientific world, Leonard Bloomfield published his book, **Language,** which provided a basis for describing and writing previously unwritten languages.

God had given W.C. Townsend a tremendous vision for the Bible in every person's language. It was time to act on that vision. In 1934, Towsend and L.L. Legters began the Summer Institute of Linguistics (also known as Camp Wycliffe) to train young people in linguistics so they could translate the Bible into all of the world's languages. Wycliffe Bible Translators was organized in 1942. Eugene Nida later promoted these linguistic principles in Bible Society circles.

Since 1934: Since 1934 pioneer translation efforts have majored in non-European languages. Literacy campaigns have been carried on simultaneously with translation efforts. The Bible Societies have increasingly worked with national believers to revise existing Scriptures and to produce "common language" versions.

Wycliffe Bible Translators and the Summer Institute of Linguistics have focused on providing Scripture for people who have never had a translation in their language. This includes (1) language groups where there are churches but no Scriptures and (2) groups where there are no churches and there is little or no understanding of the gospel. In most cases, their languages have never been written.

Is it not exciting to see the "speed" of the upward movement of the line!?? One missionary wrote the following in 1989. Thirty-three (33) percent of the world's population claimed to be Christians, like one out of three. He also mentioned that Africa, Europe and Latin America each have more Christians than North America, that only 24.5% of the world's population is unevangelized, that there are only 475 unreached peopled groups (i.e. nations). As they said, if ever there was a time when the possibility of World Evangelism was in the grasp of the Church, it is now.

VISION 2025

By the year 2025 a Bible IN EVERY LANGUAGE!
Wycliffe Associates

And this gospel of the kingdom will be preached in the whole world as a testimony to all nations and then the end will come.

Matthew 24:14

Septuagint
Some 200 years before Christ 70 scholars in Egypt translated the Old Testament from Hebrew to Greek. This translation became known as the Septuagint.

Targums
Long before Jesus was born, oral translations of scripture, called Targums, were being made in Jewish synagogues. A translator would stand beside the reader and translate the passages into the local Aramaic language. As early as 100 BC there were written Aramaic versions of the Old Testament, although most of the written versions appeared after the time of Christ.

Vulgate
In the fourth century Jerome revised an earlier Latin version of the Bible. His version, called the Vulgate, was for many centuries the only version authorized by the Roman Catholic Church. It was, therefore, the Bible of the Christian world.

200	100	0	100	200	300	400	500	600	700	800

Who have the translations been for?

Prior to 1800
The majority of Bible translators prior to 1800 were bilingual Christians who translated from another language into their own mother tongue. Jerome, for example, translated into Latin, Wycliffe into English and Luther into German. They translated for established churches which had heard the gospel long before and had been existing on foreign language Scriptures.

After 1800
Around 1800 European Protestants began to take the Good News around the world. Their mission fields were generally colonies governed by their respective countries. The Englishman William Carey, for instance, went to the British colony of India.

Increasingly, Bible translators after 1800 were missionaries who translated into languages they learned in order to preach the gospel. They used their translation for evangelism, teaching, church planting and church growth. The Bible Society movement, with its burden for Scripture distribution, coincided with this era.

After 1950
By the middle of the twentieth century, the colonial era was coming to an end. A strong worldwide movement for political independence brought many new independent nations into being. Increasingly, many of these nations are requiring that their own people take over tasks previously done by foreigners.

Today there is a need for both kinds of Bible translators—those who translate into their mother tongue and those who translate into an acquired language.

Our members continue to pioneer—learning languages in order to translate, as well as encouraging others to develop the skills and vision for Bible translation. Where there are mother tongue speakers with a vision to translate, we train them in vital linguistic and translation skills and provide consultant help. We provide similar help for speakers of national languages, such as Spanish or French, who are translating for a minority group.

Who's done the translations?

Prior to 1450
During the Middle Ages there was little vision for Scriptures in a person's mother tongue. The Roman Catholic church insisted on the use of Jerome's Latin version. It discouraged the use of Scriptures by anyone except clergy, scholars and kings, on the grounds that the unlearned would misinterpret it. Few people, even among the clergy, lawyers and kings could read. Handwritten copies of the Bible were

Bible Translation Through the Ages

by George Cowan with Carol Schatz

VISION 2025

Number of languages with at least one complete book of Scripture.

1982
1763

Around 1450
Renaissance;
Reformation;
Gutenberg's press

Around 1800
Beginning of
Protestant missions;
Bible translation as
tool in evangelism.

523

Wycliffe's Bible
John Wycliffe, an Oxford scholar, completed the first English translation of the Bible in the 1380s.

Luther's Bible
Martin Luther, German reformer, completed his translation of the Bible into German in 1534.

KJV Bible
The King James Version was published in 1611. It was translated by 54 scholars under orders from King James of England.

1934
Wycliffe Bible Translators and the Summer Institute of Linguistics training and field work began. (The organizations were formed in 1942.)

67
33

---

extremely expensive. The few translations that were produced were in the dominant languages of the ancient world, such as Latin and Coptic, and in early European languages.

After 1450

Around 1450 the climate for Bible translation changed. The Renaissance brought a new emphasis on learning, so that even the common man was encouraged to learn to read. The Reformation stressed the importance of knowing Scripture. Gutenberg's invention of a printing press with moveable type brought the price of a Bible

within the reach of ordinary people. As a result of all this, there was new interest in the translation of the Bible into the major languages of Europe.

1933—1934

The year 1933 was a landmark year for Bible translation. Spiritual and secular developments came together to make it the beginning of the modern Bible translation movement for ethnic people groups.

1) In Keswick, New Jersey, L.L. Legters reported to the Keswick conference on a trip to South America. The Lord sent an unusual burden on

the conferees to pray for unreached tribes.
2) In Keswick, England, John Savage of Peru also challenged conferees to pray for the unreached tribes. Again the Lord sent an unusual burden.
3) In the scientific world, Leonard Bloomfield published his book, **Language**, which provided a basis for describing and writing previously unwritten languages.

God had given W.C. Townsend a tremendous vision for the Bible in every person's language. It was time to act on that vision. In 1934, Townsend and L.L. Legters

began the Summer Institute of Linguistics (also known as Camp Wycliffe) to train young people in linguistics so they could translate the Bible into all of the world's languages. Wycliffe Bible Translators was organized in 1942. Eugene Nida later promoted these linguistic principles in Bible Society circles.

Since 1934

Since 1934 pioneer translation efforts have majored on non-European languages. Literacy campaigns have been carried on simultaneously with translation efforts.

The Bible Societies have increasingly worked with

national believers to revise existing Scriptures and to produce "common language" versions.

Wycliffe Bible Translators and the Summer Institute of Linguistics have focused on providing Scripture for people who have never had a translation in their language. This includes (1) language groups where there are churches but no Scriptures and (2) groups where there are no churches and there is little or no understanding of the gospel. In most cases, their languages have never been written.

CHAPTER 2

The Role of Technology

From the Time Line one can see that providing Scripture was a laborious endeavor as copies must be made by hand. The Line is very flat until God gave man the Gutenberg's press and moved John Wycliffe and Martin Luther to translate into English and German. What a gift to many of us that speak these languages! This encouraged the movement for Protestant Missionaries for evangelism. The Holy Spirit accelerated His work by using the printing press as a tool and the Line shot upward in the 1900's. This appears that the promise made in Joel 2:28-29 of His outpouring was now happening as "the end" draws near at an accelerated pace.

Communication over distances consisted of drumbeats, smoke signals, Semaphore, and the like. Many other limited means were employed through the years, but greater capabilities were required to effectively communicate as population and distant people contacts increased.

Discovery of making use of electricity in the late 1600's (1st energy utility in the US was in 1816) and then the telegraph in late 1800's. Wireless transmission with the first radio station in the United States in the 1920's revolutionized long-distance sharing of information. Light bulbs in the 1700's was an extraordinary discovery that changed and improved the life of man.

Batteries from the 1800's made operation possible of many technological instruments. The tape recorder, the airplane in 1903, and television was and is most useful. The computer and improvement in operating systems greatly increase the ability to translate and communicate the Word. Stationary satellites for worldwide contact are valuable in spreading the Gospel. Paper and new means of printing, the telephone and solar charged radios are invaluable means to undo the negative effect of the Tower of Babel.

I am sure you could add many more devices and who knows what else God will give to us to escalate the translation and propagation of the Scriptures to meet "the deadline" the Father has set!

Now one would say that all the aforementioned technological discoveries and their development was really for the purpose of making life livable and progressive for mankind. They all unite us in some way and are a boon for business and livelihood. As the world increases in population and diversity, technology makes the world smaller and more prosperous and promotes the brotherhood of man (to some extent). What a blessing from God!

But wait. These blessings are not primarily to benefit our lives in prosperity and the like. The primary purpose of them all is to enable God's people by the power of the Holy Spirit to effect the eleventh commandment of Jesus. Going to the moon for instance was the goal and when working toward that goal man received many side benefits from the required technology. In our case the enabled translation and spreading of the Word is the goal for God's giving the "communication inventions to the world," and business and mankind received the side benefits. The computer was given to aid in translation but as a side benefit it was useful to business and the livelihood of man. This is true of the airplane, great tool for God's goal, but the side benefit for fast and safe transportation is also realized. Some of the tools for sharing the Good News and moving of the line upward includes the following.

The printing press and the variety of ways to style and make plain scripture texts and their meaning today is invaluable. The materials for printing and speed of duplication (and implementing) is a boon for spreading the word. Look at what the Gutenberg Press added to the line on the graph!

The telegraph led to the telephone making distance "less of a hindrance to sharing and provided valuable contact with those involved in translating around the world. Postal service is of help in many ways of raising necessary funds and disseminating information needed for promoting the Word.

The loud speaker was first invented by Alexander Graham Bell who incorporated the device into his other inventions, the telephone. This made possible the operation of the radio, movies, records, tapes, CD's, DVD's, TV's, cell phones, and other sound equipment. Its main purpose though is to enable the preaching of the gospel to large and small audiences. This made possible the use of many devices to tell the good news. Can you imagine what it sounded like when Jesus preached to the 5000 (10,000+?) out in the open without a microphone. It must have been very quiet and a miracle.

The Facsimile allowed instant contact and information sharing.

The car phone and cellular phone with all its apps has become a real help. Here is a paragraph from Wycliffe's Bob Creson and Ken and Chris Van Weerdhuizen regarding use of a smartphone. Moise Yenta, who lives in Cameroon, read aloud a Scripture portion on his smartphone, punctuating the phrases with vigorous gestures. This was God's Word in his mother tongue – the Ngiemboon language of Cameroon – and he was seeing it on his phone for the first time! As he came to the end of the selection, he jumped up and delightedly shook hands with a colleague. With a huge grin, he exclaimed, "Wonderful! Wonderful!" He says, "I was so happy that I couldn't hide it! Immediately I applied the lesson we learned by selecting a verse and sending it to my dear wife, and she was happy to receive it."

Video conferencing, emails, and skype, twitter and text messaging are useful tools to exchange information and messages.

Radio has been one of the most effective means of communicating the Gospel throughout the world as there is practically no place on earth that cannot be reached with this means.

Here are several other ways technology is being used by many organizations for reaching out.

There are some community development people who have traveled over almost impossible terrain in Afghanistan with medical supplies and audio, solar powered Bibles, to reach people, as it were, at the farthest and most unreachable place on earth. The Holy Spirit will use these radios to open the hearts of those who live there.

Briefly then, with approximate dates:

The Postal Service (approx. 1776)
Telegraph (1794 & 1830)
Telephone (1876)
Facsimile (1970)
Car Phone (1973)
Video Conferencing (1970's)
Email (1971)
Instant messaging like Skype, google, facetime (1996)
Text Messaging (1985)
6 degrees (1997)
Twitter (2006)

These are all spectacular means of communication to help spread the Good News completely around the world. The Holy Spirit must and does go with the sent message else no one would listen or understand. There are many ways to promote use of the means God has given for moving the line. Here are several examples though there are hundreds more.

Covenant CRC in Michigan has supported a fish pond enterprise in Burundi Africa. The local people work the fishery which supply wages and food for themselves and others. The church has supplied many audio, solar powered, Bibles in their language. This is especially helpful to those who are unable to read.

Thru the Bible Broadcast has translated Dr. McGee's 5-year program going through the Bible, verse by verse, into more than 400 languages. Those broadcasts are shared around the world by radio and internet transmissions. Many pastors in many counties use his lessons to help prepare sermons. Thru the Bible program has received letters from jungle areas thanking them for their broadcast into remote places that have no minister or church.

The Harrington family in 2014, with Wycliffe Association and global ministry team, Distant Share Media, began propelling the Audio engineering critical for unfolding the Word to meet the multi-media needs of more than 5 billion people living in oral culture countries today. Many cultures are oral in communication, either no written language or not able to read the printed page. Here is where the audio devices are invaluable in presenting Jesus and His word.

Medical technology, including medicine and knowledge, is used to help many in areas of the world which have little or no healthcare. This is a great tool being used to bring Jesus to those who haven't heard.

Clean water is so needed in many underdeveloped countries and being able to help in drilling wells or in making safe water by filtration is another means used to help open the door. Contaminated water is probably the greatest killer on the planet.

One more note on significant technology. The Grand Rapids Press reported in an article on technology in July, 2016 headlined "Device aims to bring internet to the ends of the earth." Facebook launched a new piece of hardware that could be used to bring the Good News via internet to the most remote places on planet earth. Facebook calls it Open Cellular. This, of course, is its primary purpose to spread the Gospel throughout the world. The side benefits would be helpful to business, governments and personal communication. There will surely be more such technology coming to enable us to be obedient to Jesus command.

Remember this, that all technology is a tool in the hands of the Holy Spirit to bring the Word to all people and nations, to open hearts to know Jesus and to bring Him back. We then must make use of it and work with the Spirit.

The Jesus films has been an effective, dramatic success in introducing Jesus to many using an attention getting media.

The automobile, air plane and helicopter play a key role in allowing transportation that is very useful in mission and translating activity.

All media may not be used directly to minister the Word, but does help churches and organizations to communicate with one another.

CHAPTER 3

Role of the United States of America

Some have concluded that nowhere in Scripture is found any prophecy that may refer to the United States. The book of Daniel does predict the rising and fall of many good and evil powers, but our country does not appear to be included here. The only Scripture that I believe may apply is found in Revelations 18:14-18. I vision this as many countries benefited from the financial wealth and freedoms God has blessed us with but when Satan succeeds in its destruction this benefit will end for all.

Looking behind the scenes of History, we see a raging spiritual battle as the timeline moves to completion. Certainly, this battle was ongoing since the fall of Adam (Genesis 3:16) and continued until Jesus birth. Then the pursuit of the woman with child with Herod (Matthew 2:16) began and is manifest in Satan's pursuit of the Church. (Revelation 12)

The United States of America is a very unique country with a beginning similar to Biblical Israel, a country created and sustained by God for His special purpose. The constitution, though not inspired by the Holy Spirit like the scriptures, yet was surely written by men with His guidance, incorporating His desire for how men should live in freedom under God.

One detail that is seldom mentioned is that in Washington, D.C. there can never be a building of greater height than the Washington Monument. On the aluminum cap top the Washington Monument in Washington, D.C., are displayed two words: Laus Deo.

No one can see these words. In fact, most visitors to the monument are totally unaware they are even there and for that matter, probably couldn't care less. Once you know Laus Deo's history, you will want to share this with everyone you know.

These words have been there for many years; they are at 555 feet and 5.125 inches high, perched atop the monument, facing skyward to the Father of our nation, overlooking the 69 square miles which comprise the District of Columbia, capital of the United States of America. Laus Deo! Two seemingly insignificant, unnoticed words. Out of sight and, one might think, out of mind, but very meaningfully placed at the highest point over what is the most powerful city in the most successful nation in the world. So, what do those two words, in Latin, composed of just four syllables and only seven letters, possibly mean?

Very simply, they say 'Praise be to God!'

Though construction of this giant obelisk began in 1848, when James Polk was President of the United States, it was not until 1888 that the monument was inaugurated and opened to the public. It took twenty-five years to finally cap the memorial with a tribute to the Father of our nation, Laus Deo, 'Praise be to God!'

From atop this magnificent granite and marble structure, visitors may take in the beautiful panoramic view of the city with its division into four major segments. From that vantage point, one can also easily see the original plan of the designer, Pierre Charles L'Enfant….a perfect cross imposed upon the landscape, with the White House to the north, the Jefferson Memorial is to the south, the Capitol to the east and the Lincoln Memorial to the west. When the cornerstone of the Washington Monument was laid on July 4th 1848 deposited within it were many items including the Holy Bible presented by the Bible Society. Praise be to God! Such was the discipline, the moral direction, and the spiritual mood given by the founder and first President. Here is George Washington's prayer for America…."Almighty God; We make our earnest prayer that Thou wilt keep the United States in Thy holy protection/ that Thou wilt incline the hearts of the citizens to cultivate a spirit of subordination and obedience to government; and entertain a brotherly affection and love for one another and for their fellow citizens of the United States at large. And finally that Thou wilt most graciously be pleased to dispose us all to do justice, to love MERCY, and to demean ourselves with that charity, humility, and pacific temper of mind which were the characteristics of the Divine Author of our blessed religion, and without a humble imitation of whose example in these things we can never hope to be a happy nation.

Grant supplication, we beseech Thee, through Jesus Christ our Lord.

Amen."

Laus Deo!

Richard N. Ostling of the Associated Press wrote an article headlined "Christianity gets credit for Wests freedom, sociologists claims". He is referring to Professor Rodney Stark of Baylor University. What Mr. Ostling writes is the following.

It's one of history's most important questions: Why did Europe and North America embrace democracy and thrive economically while nations elsewhere suffered oppression and stagnation? Leading U.S. sociologist Rodney Stark says many scholars purposely overlook the obvious answer: It was the spread of Christianity that made possible political and economic freedoms, modern science and resulting advancement.

Such is the Baylor University professor's contention in "The Victory of Reason: How Christianity Led to Freedom, Capitalism and Western Success" (Random House), one of the more provocative of recent books. Although Western intellectuals downplay theology, Stark sees Christian beliefs as the key.

I agree with this understanding which emphasizes, the role of the United States, a plan and blessing of God. What a privilege this country has!

Look at the way the US dealt with its defeated enemies in all wars, often making allies of them for mutual gain. It is a fact that its military is the only major force that keeps chaos from occurring in the world. This is of God, of course, who has blessed this land because of His purpose for it. It is well known that this land was settled by many who left their homelands for religious freedom. They fled religious persecution and based their hope in God, coming here to build a life in Him. Many of the Founding Fathers were Christians and spoke openly of God's purpose for the county and founded on Judeo Christian values. The Constitution was written to preserve religious freedom. Many of those involved in the early days spoke of our God's involvement and how important it was for the country to follow His laws. Even up to this day there are many in government, though more of a minority now, that confess His name. Religious freedom for Christians and the Constitution is under attack. The clause that states "freedom of religion" is being interpreted "freedom from religion". This helped ban the Bible or teaching from it in the public schools, government offices, and some businesses.

Those who settled and built this country were not without sin but were used to construct a country that governed with Christian values and centered laws. The country was then blessed and prospered with a capitalistic economy and offered freedom and justice for its citizens. Our fallen nature had to be overcome to do this. The USA was appointed then to spread the Gospel throughout the world using its wealth and Christian good will to those in need.

As evidence of this, for many years this country gave economic assistance to 103 needy countries. In 2011, military assistance was 17.8 billion and economic aid was 71.2 billion. In the year 2012 the US spent 37.7 billion dollars in foreign aid. This does not cover cost of past wars that were to keep order and freedom for people. On October 5, 1947, in the first televised White House address, President Truman asked Americans to refrain from eating meat on Tuesdays and poultry on Thursdays to help stockpile grains for starving people in Europe.

A report on this country's donations was given in a 2016 article from money tips.com entitled "Who's helping charities in a generous America?" Charitable giving is making a recovery after the hit it took during the Great Recession. Here are a few facts about America's recent charitable giving. Charity Navigator notes that total gifts to charity in 2013 reached more than $335 billion, continuing the trend for four straight years of increased giving with a 4.4 percent jump. Record-setting giving in 2014 ($358.38 billion) and 2015 ($373.25 billion) beat the pre-recession (2007) mark of $349.5 billion. According to the National Philanthropic Trust, the vast majority of us participate in some sort of charitable giving – a whopping 98.4 percent of high-net-worth households in 2013. Many of these contributions are small, but the average household contribution is a respectable $2,974. Individual spirit still drives our charity. Seventy-one percent of our giving ($268.28 billion) came from individuals, with the remainder contributed by foundations, bequests and corporations (16, 9, and 5 percent, respectively).

Another article reports that a third of charitable contributions go to churches or other religious organizations, and that sector is the single biggest beneficiary of charitable giving. Nationwide religious organizations rank number one in total donations received by nonprofits, according to Giving USA, an organization that tracks charitable contributions.

From World War I until now it is evident the countries of the world depended on the United States for peace and prosperity. As a young boy I would search out in the newspaper the many countries given financial aid to help feed their people and create stability. This continues today. Though in many cases distribution was not handled properly by the US or the recipients.

Romans 12:20 says "If your enemy is hungry, feed him, if he is thirsty, give him something to drink." This is what the United States has done in WWI and WWII and other conflicts. One more proof that the Holy Spirit has purposed our county to keep peace and use the wealth and freedom to bring Jesus to all nations. What a privilege!

Our country was and is not one without many faults and committed many errors over time. This is a fallen world. Its founding basis was religious freedom based on trust in Jesus Christ. Over time its trust in the living God has decreased to a dangerous level. The Christian influence has made it unique. After winning the two world wars it built up those defeated countries. It did not try to take them over and plunder them as other victorious powers did in the past. Before dropping atomic bombs on Japan, millions of leaflets were delivered in warning. It's involvement in other wars like Korea, Vietnam, and in the Mid-East did allow the Gospel to enter by means of some Christian soldiers and Christian organizations that went there to help the people.

Though slavery existed throughout history (Israel enslaved 400 years) the enslaving of Africans with the help of the Dutch and Africans themselves was wrong and we continue to pay a big price for this evil. But today I have millions of African Christian brothers and sisters living here. I am sure many have returned to bring the Good news to their people. This is true of Americans treatment of the Indians also as being infected with original sin and its consequences, many mistakes were made. God did want this country settled by His people but it should have been done in a way that honors Him. He did bring many Indians into His house and continues to do so today.

In past history there was this phrase "the sun never sets on the British empire". Now that sounds like a nation seeking its own prosperity at the expense of other nations. Granted, some conquerors would kill off the entire population, but Britain was more of a blessing in that regard. God had a different plan for the British as they were instrumental in bringing the Gospel to many nations.

So now you can see how man did things that were evil but God used them to do good by bringing life to many people. As mentioned earlier the United States was involved in destructive behavior but God used contact with other nations as a means to bring in the Good News.

Along with this, I believe that the "white people" will be minorities in Heaven. God often turns evil into good. All praise to Him!

Now back to the role of the United States in God's plan. You can understand from the last paragraph that I am not trying to make it look like our country is so good and great in itself and that is why He blesses us, but God is still using it for His purpose.

What is its purpose or assignment? The United States has been blessed as He is using its attributes in the final years of History to spread the Gospel. We have the assignment and command to pressure the line on the cover to completion. God has many people, many churches, here that are doing this work. Our freedoms and prosperity, though our prayers are often asking God to let us keep them, is not for our pleasure. It is given to enable the spread of the Gospel, and not so we would have a nice life. That good life is a side benefit resulting from the main purpose.

A unique responsibility and blessing God has given to the United States is the technology listed in Chapter 4. The discovery and production of technological inventions to enable the spread of the Gospel worldwide was largely given to this county. Prosperity and freedom, plus its Christian citizens allowed discovery, development and uses of those gifts. As a side benefit business could use and people could enjoy them.

In the History of the United States it is evident there were always forces to destroy it, either from outside or by some of its own people. The major events were WWI and WWII. Satan could see that this country was given the resources and power to spread the Word and knows his time is up when the "line" on the cover is complete. These efforts were not successful. Protection of Israel, God's people, is assigned to us. He still loves them and we owe them, as our Jesus is Jewish and He came according to His promise. It amazes me, yet it shows God's love for Israel and His protective power, that being surrounded by many countries that openly talk of annihilating them, Israel is still there!

The United States military is appointed by God to maintain peace to help spread the Gospel through the world. Its power was not to be used to conquer like other countries did in part but to enable fulfilment of the prophecy that Jesus will return after the Word is in every part of the world. <u>Because the purpose of the United States and its power, freedom, and financial blessing are for the propagation of the Gospel, I believe that all those who served, died in battle or were injured in defending our country, for this, God will take that into account as credit in the judgement day. If unbelievers at the time he could give salvation to those people or lessen their punishment in hell. They gave their lives for the Gospel sake so Memorial Day is special to God and to us.</u>

Satan, then has tried to destroy the US with world wars and afterward tried communism. He tried to break the country's spirit with terrorism beginning with the 911 fear and violence. The attack on the Trade Center represented the economy, on the Pentagon, the military power that protects the country, its allies and the world, and the crashing of the plane in Shanksville, Pennsylvania, the citizens of the United States. These methods did not work. He now has two more ways to do this. Destroy us financially which also damages the world economies and to work from inside our country using bad politicians, immorality, and the church. We are still at war.

There are increasing instances of attacks on Christianity as the constitution is changed from "freedom of religion "to" freedom from religion". This allows the devil to replace Christianity with "no religion" which really is his religion. So, the devil is finding out that the best way to destroy the country appointed to move the line upward, is from the inside. It is employing the principle of the Trojan Horse. You attack from the inside in such a way that it goes unnoticed due to its gradual nature.

At this time the church does not yet see the spiritual battle raging in this country. It prays for better government and for prosperity and freedom, but does not see that with our demise the cause of Christ will be hindered. Imagine our country totally rejecting God, bringing into it Muslim and other false religions, the negative effect that it would have on pushing the Line. The world would be in chaos and would resemble the description in Matthew (and other parts of Scripture) of end times.

The election process we are in and the appointment of Supreme Court judges and others in authority will determine the world future. Again, the church views all this as politics and does not see it as part of the spiritual battle. The church speaks out less on sins clearly given in Scripture in order to be politically correct. It no longer dares to say "this is what God says". For instance, it made no defense of the Word of God versus the word of the evil one before the Supreme Court when discussing marriage or homosexuality. Nor does it contend with evolutionist which can be readily proven to be as false as a "flat earth".

Now 2020 is a very critical election year for this US being a leader of the free world. Will we see those who favor immorality, decline of Christianity, corruption, and suppression of freedom and prosperity run or will God's people contend for Him and fight these evils for the sake of the spread of the Word in spite of the persecution that will come? Satan is right. The best way to destroy the United States is to do it from the inside. It is working for him today!

Chapter 5 will explain another major cause for its purpose and power. Support for Israel, the people whom God loves and from where our Savior came from, was waning in the Washington political environment. The United

States is appointed to protect Israel. It amazes me that this small country, surrounded by countries that want to destroy her, are powerless to do this at this time. *President Trump stated at the U.S. Holocaust Memorial Museum's National Commemoration of the Days of Remembrance event at the U.S. Capitol on Tuesday, April 25, 2017: "This is my pledge to you: We will confront anti-Semitism. We will stamp out prejudice. We will condemn hatred. We will bear witness, and we will act. As president of the United States, I will always stand with the Jewish people, and I will always stand with our great friend and partner, the state of Israel." *Jewish Voice Today Magazine 3rd quarter 2018

At the time of this writing there is increasing violence and unrest as Satan is trying to destroy the United States. With his people he is unrelentlessly attacking the elected president and his supporters. Most of the accusations are lies and include unprecedented personal, hostile actions and words to injure or discredit. God put this president in office and Satan and his people are angry with God. He says in Daniel 5:21c "until Nebuchadnezzar acknowledged that the most High God is sovereign over the kingdoms of men and sets over them anyone He wishes.

The previous administration left behind many of its people who criminally sought to undermine the election and other misdeeds. Some of those involved will go to prison.

Fortunately, there are Bible studies in the White House and many do pray over the President. He is also surrounded by Christian advisors. The Vice President is a Christian and the President is not afraid to use the name of our God, Jesus. He was the first President to speak at the Right to Life assembly in Washington DC. Because of God's protection and enabling power the president is able to withstand the constant personal attacks on him, his wife, and his family.

I am not the only one who opines God's reason for making Donald Trump President of the Untied States. Christian End Times prepper Jim Bakker said that God told him He put Donald Trump on this earth to give the church time to prepare for the impending end.

Bakker said, "There is such hatred for the gospel. This is the Antichrist spirit loose," and for this reason, "God has given us a man who is not afraid to fight. We have a president people think is crazy. They call him crazy, but he's making peace treaties, he's doing all the things to try to solve the world's problems and God has put him on earth-God spoke to me the other night, He said, "I put Donald Trump on earth to give you time, the church, to get ready." He said, "Donald Trump is a respite in his troubled times, and I sent him in grace to give you time to prepare for what's coming on earth."

In March of 2019 President Trump issued a proclamation officially recognizing Israeli sovereignty over the Golan Heights, an elevated defense position for Israel's safety. Could God be using this act, plus the others that the President has done for Israel, be in preparation for Jesus return to Jerusalem?

The actions of this President is causing more antisemitism and hatred by Satan's people as "The Day" approaches. They are trying to stop this "Day!"

President Trump does show his support for Christians in that he was the only President at Billy Graham funeral. Also, the White House hosted a dinner on August 27 for about 100 evangelical Christian leaders and senior-level officials, honoring evangelicals, as one participant explained, "for all the good work they do."

Calling America "a nation of believers," President Trump said at the event that they had gathered to "celebrate America's heritage of faith, family, and freedom."

"As you know, in recent years the government tried to undermine religious freedom, but the attacks on communities of faith are over," the president said. "We've ended it. We've ended it. Unlike some before us, we are protecting your religious liberty."

In May 2018, the President, in a Rose Garden ceremony, announced an executive order he said would expand government grants to and partnerships with faith-based groups.

President Donald Trump told attendees at the annual National Prayer Breakfast that he stands behind them, even as speakers bemoaned the level of division in the country and what one described as a "fracturing of the American family." I will never let you down," Trump told an audience that included members of his Cabinet and Congress. The pledge came two days after Trump offered a fierce denunciation of late-term abortion in his annual State of the Union address as he moved to re-energize evangelical voters, who have been among his most loyal supporters. "We must build a culture that cherishes the dignity and sanctity of innocent human life," Trump said, adding that: "All children, born and unborn, are made in the holy image of God." "As president I will always cherish, honor and protect the believers who uplift our communities and sustain our nation," he said. Guatemala's ambassador to the U.S., Manual Espina, offered prayers for Trump, saying: "We pray that you'll give him the wisdom and the knowledge to lead this county under your principles and guidance."

Also, President Donald Trump gave his blessing to lawmakers in several states who are pushing legislation to allow Bible literacy classes in public schools. "Numerous states introducing Bible Literacy classes, giving students the option of studying the Bible," Trump wrote in a morning tweet. "Starting to make a turn back? Great!"

Can one not see that the increasing attacks on the President, on Christians and their values, and on our nations stability is a result of Satan's attempt to destroy the United States as it's people, freedom, and economy is being used to bring the Word to every nation by 2025? This is the Trojan Horse method being used to destroy and is promoted by social media.

A top faith advisor to Trump said the aim was a culture change producing less conversations about church-state barriers "without all these arbitrary concerns as to what is appropriate."

In December 2018, President George HW Bush went home to his Lord and Savior. His funeral was a testimony of God's presence in his life and a witness to all who attended or watched it in the media. The service gave opportunity to know Him. The fact that God put him in as President again shows His plan for using the United States as a special country to enable the spread of the Gospel.

Recognizing, Jerusalem as Israel's capital and plans to move there in 2019 is causing strong displeasure here and among those surrounding countries of Israel that have vowed to destroy her. However, in Genesis 12:3 God says "I will bless those who bless you, and all the peoples on earth will be blessed through you." This is fulfilled in Jesus coming from the Jewish peoples.

Why is Jerusalem so important? Here is some information from a Zondervan Bible Dictionary about Jerusalem.

Jerusalem, in the history of God's revelation to man in those Divine acts by which redemption has been accomplished, by far the most important site on this earth. It was the royal city, the capital of the only kingdom God has (thus far) established among men; here the temple was erected and here alone, during the kingdom age, were sacrifices legitimately offered. This was the city of the prophets, as well as the kings of David's line. Here occurred the death, resurrection and ascension of Jesus Christ, David's greatest Son. Upon an assembled group in this city the Holy Spirit descended at Pentecost, giving birth to the Christian Church, and here the first great Church council was held. Rightly did the chronicler refer to Jerusalem as the "city which Jehovah had chosen out of all the tribes of Israel to put his name there" (I Kings 14:21). Even the Roman historian Pliny of the first century, referred to Jerusalem as "by far the most famous city of the ancient orient" (H.N.V.14). This city has been the preeminent objective of the pilgrimages of devout men and women for over 2,000 years, and it was in an attempt to recover the Church of the Holy Sepulcher in Jerusalem that all the Crusades were organized.

No site in all the Scriptures receives such constant and exalted praise as Jerusalem. No place in the world have such promises been made of ultimate glory and permanent peace. The city close to God's heart is Jerusalem and is mentioned 471 times in the Scriptures.

Jewish tradition has identified Mount Moriah as Jerusalem where Abraham was to sacrifice his only son, Isaac, the only son Abraham had with Sarah. He, through Isaac, God's promise to Abraham was fulfilled. John 3:16 says "For God so loved the world that He gave His one and only Son." Jesus is the fulfillment of God's promise to the Jews and the world. The hill at Jerusalem is where Solomon built the "House of the Lord", the Temple. The temple was built on the threshing floor of Ornan (2 Chronicles 3:17) where David was told to build an altar for sacrifices for his greatest sin, namely, of numbering the people of Israel. The Jews believe the altar of burnt offering in the Temple, at Jerusalem was situated on the exact site where Abraham intended to sacrifice Isaac. The Dome of the Rock, the Muslim mosque, presently is situated on this site. Now the presence of the Muslim Dome on the Rock presents a serious problem. Israel is surrounded by hostile nations and removing the Dome may be the setting up of the scene described by Jesus in Matthew 24:15. Can you see that we may well be living in the final days of earth's history?

Jerusalem was always a special place for Jews, and later, Christians. In Genesis 14:18 it was known as Salem where Abram (later Abraham) met Melchizedek. It was also known as Jebus and later the city of David after he took it from the Jebusites. David made it the religious capital of Israel. Solomon built the temple there and it was destroyed in 587 B.C. by Nebuchadnezzar. The people were scattered, and they grieved for the Holy City, also referred to as Zion in Psalm 137:1. The temple was rebuilt several times and finally destroyed by the Romans after Jesus ascended. It was no longer needed.

Jesus was born in Bethlehem, about 5 miles from Jerusalem. Joseph and Mary brought Him to the Temple to be dedicated to the Lord. He spent a lot of time in that city and wept over it (Matthew 23:37). After the judgment day, John, in Revelation says he saw a new heaven and earth, the Holy City, The New Jerusalem coming down out of Heaven (Revelation 21:22). The New Testament church in Jerusalem played a significant role in the early spread of Christianity. It is where Christianity began. It became a Holy City for both the Jewish and Gentile Christians. One can see that this particular area of the world still has a special place in God's heart. It is where His chosen people whom He loves and is gathering just as He promised. Deuteronomy 12:5, Psalms 87:2 and Psalm 132:14

What do modern day Jews think about Jerusalem today? Israel first Prime Minister, David Ben-Gurion, on December 5, 1949, stated that "Jerusalem is an inseparable part of Israel and her eternal capital. No United Nations vote can alter this historical fact." He said this only days after the UN voted for a resolution rallying for internationalization of Jerusalem.

I believe one more major occurrence must take place and that is the making of Jerusalem a complete property of Israel. God has to do this as the area is populated by Muslims and the Dome on the Rock is there, a stronghold of Satan.

Though there is violence, in response to the President of the United States decision, we hope and pray as it is meant to be, a way to bring peace to the area. This would help the Jewish people as a nation turn to Jesus and allow the Good News, by the power of the Holy Spirit, to turn the hearts of all surrounding nations to Him. It would be wonderful to see Israel become a Christian nation! In Isaiah 2:2-3 He says "In the last days the law will go out from Zion, the word of the Lord from Jerusalem."

I believe this is the final assignment and responsibility of the United States of America. Deuteronomy 30:3-4, Isaiah 11:11-12 and Jeremiah 16:14-15 and Ezekiel 39:25-29, God promises to bring the Jewish people back to their own country from the four corners of the earth where they were scattered. There is no country as blessed by God that is able to help in this task, one of the final signs the blindness of Jews may now be removed as a nation.

This was, in part, confirmed by the President of the United States of America in his first State of the Union message on January 30, 2018. He said we must be strong to keep peace in the world <u>and trust in our God.</u> He also said <u>we are one nation under God.</u> Then, importantly, he pointed out that we recognize Jerusalem as Israel's capital. This significant sign occurred in December, 2017 when President Trump made the decision regarding Jerusalem. We know God put the man whom He chooses, to be president, either to test the church or enable it to do its work.

This comes from and is only accomplished by the power of our Father, our Jesus, and Holy Spirit, the one and only true God.

The president of the International Fellowship of Christian and Jews, Yael Eckstein wrote "Something incredible – something prophetic – happened just one year ago today when President Donald Trump moved the American embassy to God's eternal city of Jerusalem on Israel's 70th anniversary!" I know who's really responsible for something this big and this important! Since Israel declared her independence in 1948, <u>Christians in America and around the world</u> have remained steadfast in their support for God's chosen people. You've made your support known to your loved ones, your churches, your communities-even your government. And because of you, God is doing big things. Its not just me who see your bravery, support, and strength – Israelis everywhere know <u>that Christians</u> are the very best friends of Israel and <u>the Jewish people.</u>

I would like to add two more signs that point to Jesus's soon return in addition to moving the line on the graph.

The amazing benefit we have in the Western World is the complete Scripture (Word of life) available in many languages and to anyone who wants it. This was not true from Adam until beginning with the printing press and almost fully obtainable with the help of technology. This is surely unprecedented and may be one item from the sign of increased knowledge.

One more sign, a subject covered in Chapter 4, is the recognition of Jerusalem as the capital of the nation Israel. It will take 6-8 years to complete the move from Tel Aviv. This happening is related to the information quoted earlier in the Chapter from "The Jewish Voice".

As mentioned before, could this be the setting up for the final event in Matthew 24:3, Jerusalem destruction due to Israel's disagreeing, neighboring nations?

God is protecting her until the end times advice Jesus gives to Judea in Mathew 24:15-16. [15] "So when you see standing in the holy place 'the abomination that causes desolation,'[a] spoken of through the prophet Daniel— let the reader understand— [16] then let those who are in Judea flee to the mountains.

Chapter 6 will also illustrate the purpose for economic prosperity and the presence of the Holy Spirit in action. The Levites were not given land and possessions, so we must not be clinging too much but use the gifts for Him. Yet the Levites got something infinitely better, for God said "Jehovah was their inheritance!" Let that be our reward.

Let me emphasize again how important the United States is in Gods plan and for all to no longer look at events here as political but see it as part of the raging spiritual battle.

When Jesus came to earth to fulfill the promises in the Old Testament the Roman Empire was in existence. This Empire kept order in a large part of the known world. Jesus chose 12 disciples and Christian missions began. Persecutions made Christians leave their homes and the Good News went with them. The power of the poured out Holy Spirit enabled His people and the apostle Paul to make mission journeys to many countries.

The United States is similar in purpose to the Roman Empire. That ancient force produced and kept order in much of the civilized world as the United States is doing today. This enabling force is worldwide today so Matthew 24:14 will be effected. The presidential election of the year 2020 will either give missions more time or begin the time of more persecutions of Christians in the United States and hardship given in Matthew 24. So now we are able to see related historical happenings that result in the greatest events in the history of the world and the universe. We saw mission enabling order from the Roman Empire and now experience the similar role for the United States of America. We saw Jesus come to earth the first time and many living today will see His second and final return.

In a paper written by Rachel Evans titled Why Millennials are Leaving the Church she gives one of the reasons as follows. "Armed with the latest surveys, along with personal testimonies from friends and readers, I explain how young adults perceive evangelical Christianity to be too political, too exclusive, old-fashioned, unconcerned with social justice and hostile to lesbian, gay, bisexual and transgender people." As God's people you must see the reason for this finding and the turmoil here and in the world is caused by Satan's people as he is trying to stop the line on the graph. He is finished when Jesus returns. Our freedom and prosperity is for spreading the Gospel and that purpose alone! If the United States is destroyed, which nation will do the work? China, Russia, England, France, or Mexico? Can you see what I am saying here? The United States and Israel will be destroyed as the line is completed but now we must unite and use our blessings for such a purpose and time as this!

If the opposition was in power now, ministers in our church would be forced to do situations the Bible forbids. They would be forced out of the ministry. We would no longer protect Israel. This country always welcomed legal immigration but the opposition wants to flood this country with illegals, gangs, antichristian, drug suppliers, the sex trade and the like. Our morals and economy would soon collapse which would prevent support of worldwide missions.

If this were allowed now, persecution would be in full force. This will increase so everyone, especially the young people must prepare spiritually. It could begin in the year 2020 as the Word of God is almost throughout the whole world -to the Gentiles- and the Messianic Jews are increasing dramatically in Israel. These two events must take place before He returns.

CHAPTER 4

Signs of the Times.

The longing of God's people is to see the appearing of His promised Son, Jesus. When we are young we look forward to our exciting life in this world which dims the desire to see Jesus's return and also are affected by events around us. But as we age the hope and its intensity grows.

This promised Savior told us to "read the fig tree" (Matthew 24:32-33) and eagerly look at the given signs as to the time of harvest. He is telling us who live on this side of the Cross to get prepared for His return.

The signs may appear open ended, as no definite day can be determined by the signs. This is purposeful and wise on God's part because to know the exact date would make us careless in our daily living. If we were given a date of say 10 years from now we would feel we have 9 years or plenty of time to get serious. The given signs do excite us though as we see them intensify in history

Now it is difficult to see prophesy fulfilled in ones life. For the disciples to understand that Jesus is the Promised Messiah it took the full ministry of Jesus to take place before they believed. It is much easier to look back to discern what truly took place as was predicted in the Old Testament. It is easier for us to see the completion of the promises of His first coming compared to the disciples. In spite of the miraculous events for those living at that time (and even until now) they said "where is the promise of His coming?" I believe that even if the signs and wonders were happening in our day, many would look for a scientific answer to any phenomenon. It is of course, the Holy Spirit that helps us read the signs, giving understanding of the Scriptures.

The signs do create an excitement for His people who long to see Him. Many signs appear to be in progress and may make it look like Jesus will soon be back! The disciples and early Christians opined that Jesus will return in their life time. This view certainly makes one more responsible to always be ready for His return.

Many times, in modern history, books have been written picking the day and/or the year of Jesus return. However, in Matthew 24:36, He says that "no one but the Father knows that day and hour". He did not know it at that time because He "emptied Himself" when He left Heaven to save His people. But He did give signs of the end. His most defining statement is found in Matthew 24:14. [14] "And this gospel of the kingdom will be preached in the whole world as a testimony to all nations, and then the end will come".

The apostles knew of the prophecies in Daniel and other Old Testament sources. They were convinced even at that time He was coming soon. They asked Jesus about this as recorded in Matthew 24. I believe, as is especially true today, that end times interest is the most exciting subject for God's people then and now. Jesus told us to read the signs in Matthew 24:32 and Mark 13:28-29 and to share this with everyone.

The Word of God is the only authority and source of signs of His return. Following are the ones He has given in Scripture.

Matthew 24:3 - ³ As Jesus was sitting on the Mount of Olives, the disciples came to him privately. "Tell us," they said, "when will this happen, and what will be the sign of your coming and of the end of the age?"

Jerusalem will be destroyed, not one stone will be left on another.

⁵ For many will come in my name, claiming, 'I am the Messiah,' and will deceive many.

⁶ You will hear of wars and rumors of wars, but see to it that you are not alarmed. Such things must happen, but the end is still to come.

¹⁰ Then he said to them: "Nation will rise against nation, and kingdom against kingdom. ¹¹ There will be great earthquakes, famines and pestilences in various places, and fearful events and great signs from heaven.

⁹ "Then you will be handed over to be persecuted and put to death, and you will be hated by all nations because of me. ¹⁰ At that time many will turn away from the faith and will betray and hate each other, ¹¹ and many false prophets will appear and deceive many people. ¹² Because of the increase of wickedness, the love of most will grow cold, ¹³ but the one who stands firm to the end will be saved.

In a special report of February, 2018 the American Bible Society addressed this sign. It states that Christians around the world are being targeted by persecution more than ever. In fact there are many places on earth where being a Christian is the most dangerous thing you can be. Amazingly, as dangers grows, so do requests for Bibles. These brave and courageous believers are pleading for a Bible in a language they can understand and relate to. Persecution of believers happens on every single continent. Worldwide estimates indicate the 215 million Christians experienced high or extreme levels of persecution last year in 50 countries where it is most difficult to be a follower of Jesus Christ. American Bible Society's answer is to support those believers wherever the attacks are mounting and whatever the scope. The impact is powerful.

Matthew 24:15-29, Mark 13:14-24, Luke 21:18-26

¹⁵ "So when you see standing in the holy place 'the abomination that causes desolation,'[a] spoken of through the prophet Daniel—let the reader understand— ¹⁶ then let those who are in Judea flee to the mountains. ¹⁷ Let no one on the housetop go down to take anything out of the house. ¹⁸ Let no one in the field go back to get their cloak. ¹⁹ How dreadful it will be in those days for pregnant women and nursing mothers! ²⁰ Pray that your flight will not take place in winter or on the Sabbath. ²¹ For then there will be great distress, unequaled from the beginning of the world until now and never to be equaled again.

How could such disaster be over the whole world? There have been many wars in the past, some localized and even worldwide wars, but there was always a recovery.

Well, in March of 2018, the Russian President boasted about Russian nuclear might and confirmed a long-feared doomsday device. The weapon is an underwater torpedo that has a nuclear warhead, probably a "dirty type," that releases maximum radiation. The torpedo exploding off shore could spread radiation and render large swaths of earth uninhabitable. They also told of five (5) new weapon systems that can defeat US missile defenses. If these weapons were to be used the US would of course fire back. Life on this planet would be destroyed and no one would want to live in such an environment. So one can see that many forces are in place to effect the greatest stress coming, that Jesus will shorten those days because they are so terrible.

In August of 2018, news has come out regarding superweapon technology that will make nuclear weapons obsolete. This weapon is unstoppable as it travels at speeds of 15,000 miles per hour. Detection and interception is all but impossible. This will change world wars and world order as China, Russia, and the United States work feverishly to out distance each other. The terrible times that will come will now cover the whole world and not just part of it. This is the beginning of another sign of His prediction and return.

29 "Immediately after the distress of those days

"'the sun will be darkened,
    and the moon will not give its light;
the stars will fall from the sky,
    and the heavenly bodies will be shaken.'[b]

30 "Then will appear the sign of the Son of Man in heaven. And then all the peoples of the earth[a] will mourn when they see the Son of Man coming on the clouds of heaven, with power and great glory.[b]

32 "Now learn this lesson from the fig tree: As soon as its twigs get tender and its leaves come out, you know that summer is near. 33 Even so, when you see all these things, you know that it[a] is near, right at the door.

What signs that God has given to alert us to His return that are quite clear today? Wars and rumors of wars are now on a world-wide scale and the nuclear weapons made it possible to create fears and worldwide distribution! Famines, pestilence and earthquakes have always been present but are increasing. With larger population, floods, weather variations, and famines are growing. Pestilence like tuberculosis, rheumatic fever, STD's and diseases caused by antibiotic resistant strains are worldwide and often are gaining on efforts to stop them. Could the current coronavirus with threat of world wide disease and potential financial collapse be the actual or a precursor of what will happen in the end times.

In II Timothy 3:1-5 Paul gives another sign of Jesus return by giving a clear picture of society today. Because of social media we are more aware of what the behavior of people exists today. "But mark this, there will be terrible times in the last days. People will be lovers of themselves, lovers of money, boastful, proud, abusive, disobedient to their parents, ungrateful, unholy, without love, unforgiving, slanderous, without self-control, brutal, not lovers of the good, treacherous, rash, conceited, lovers of pleasure rather that lovers of God, having a form of godliness but denying its powers. Have nothing to do with them.

Regarding "have nothing to do with them" means do not fellowship with those who do not love God. You must talk with them and witness to them about Jesus, His love, and salvation in Him, but do not join them in sinful behavior. In the Parable of the Sower, the seed being sown is good but will not grow if it is sown in bad, thorny, or shallow soil. The bad soil is what is described here in II Timothy so we must not take part in such evil.

Now these sins have been present since the fall of man, but it seems more evident as we hear and virtually witness them on television and other media. Of course, there is more of this evil as the world's population increases. We ourselves are guilty and need the shield of the Holy Spirit to not take part in any of it.

Some statistics report that since 2009-2016 over 22 million have died from HIV/AIDS. Over 42 million people are living with HIV/AIDS. There are 14,000 new infections every day.

Regarding earthquakes, many writings report increased activity, but some dispute this claim. Several parameters exist such as areas affected, number of people killed, amount of destruction, and size as measured on the Richter Scale.

Another sign is the "fulfillment" of the Gentiles or the gospel is to every town, tribe and nation. Romans 11:25

Luke 21:24 – Jerusalem will be trampled on by the Gentiles until the time of the Gentiles is fulfilled.

[24] "They will fall by the sword and will be taken as prisoners to all the nations. Jerusalem will be trampled on by the Gentiles until the times of the Gentiles are fulfilled," which is the good news is to everyone on Earth.

Regarding Paul, God tells Ananias in Acts 9:15, "Go! This man is my chosen instrument to proclaim my name to the Gentiles ". This is really when the Gospel was given to the Gentiles and will continue until all have heard throughout the whole world. Then Jesus will return. The Prophet Joel (In Joel 2:28-32) speaks of the day of His return in the time of His Spirit being poured out on all peoples, all "types". He now uses men, woman, young and old, boys and girls to form a militant army of God to bring the Good News to all people of the world. This will drive the graph on the front of this book to completion as both Jew and Gentile will hear of Jesus. Then He will return.

Regarding, the sign of the outpouring of the Holy Spirit, we see today He is not limited by gender or age. There are many women in spiritual leadership today, ministering from the pulpit, on the mission field, leading Bible studies and many other spiritual activities. This began when the two Mary's went to Jesus empty tomb. The angel there gave them the message and they immediately went to tell the disciples. Peter found the empty tomb but told no one that day. Again, the Samaritan woman at the well met Jesus and immediately told the people that the Messiah was there. The whole city came to know Jesus because of her.

We often receive stories from Mission India, telling of little children who attended their Bible classes and being used by the Holy Spirit to bring their whole family to God. Some of the families are in troubled circumstances and are healed when they turn to Christ.

Age for witnessing and sharing your faith is not a limiting factor to the Holy Spirit. Young and old are equally as "powerful" in their witness.

Some will claim to be Jesus or a follower of Him but teaching a different gospel. Paul addresses that in Galatians 1:8-9. [8] But even if we or an angel from heaven should preach a gospel other than the one we preached to you, let them be under God's curse! [9] As we have already said, so now I say again: If anybody is preaching to you a gospel other than what you accepted, let them be under God's curse! There are some today that speak of Christ but deny His Godhead – He is very God of very God! This denial is to give a semblance of Biblical teaching but denies it's power. This is from the deceiver.

Persecution occurs in most of the world and hatred for Christ and His children are expanding. Christians are beheaded or shot in Muslim countries, beaten and imprisoned by many others. On, June 27, 2019, some Islamists in Burkina Faso forced everyone in a village to lie face down on the ground. They searched each one and found four Christians wearing crucifixes. They were killed. Terrorism worldwide is prevalent today as Satan is trying to stop the growth of "the graph," or in other words the spread of the Gospel.

Anti-Semitism is increasing all over the world even in the United States, including many who are seeking government office today. This is unprecedented.

Many will turn away, betray and hate one another. Every day the news will report murders or abuse by family members against their family. Love will grow cold which is more evident than 30 years ago.

Suicides and death by overdose of opioids are more numerous at an alarming rate. Without Jesus there is only pain and a deep dark void.

As it was in the days of Noah before the flood, every imagination of the thoughts of their heart was only evil continually (Genesis 6:5). ⁵ The LORD saw how great the wickedness of the human race had become on the earth, and that every inclination of the thoughts of the human heart was only evil all the time. God was patient with them as it took years for Noah to build the ark. Man is approaching this lifestyle. Since World War II liberalization of churches in Europe and in America has occurred, slowing the process of "going into all of the world".

The Prophet Daniel in Chapter 12 writes of the end times and in answer to this question God gives little information. He is told of times of unprecedented stress, the resurrection of the dead to salvation or the second death. This, of course is before the birth and resurrection and ascension of Jesus to heaven. He was told that knowledge will increase which means Jesus being revealed and also scientific knowledge (Daniel 12:4). More Biblical prophecies are being fulfilled and technology is expanding. * "We live in the information age and some have said that 90% of all the scientist who ever lived are alive today". This "knowledge" is given for the purpose of spreading the Gospel.

The abomination of desolation has been identified in a variety of persons and religions. There seems to be disagreements as to who or what this is that leaves that sign without a definite answer. It is described by some as the antichrist, a single person. Antiochus of 175-165 BC killed many Jews and defiled the Temple in Jerusalem. The Romans, under Titus, destroyed the Temple leaving "not one stone on another." They also killed many Jews. The Islamic Shrine, the Dome of the Rock (the abomination of desolation) with its declarations that God has no Son and Jesus is not God. They killed hundreds of thousands of Jews like the Romans and then took over Jerusalem. Sacrifices ended for the Jews because Jesus made that practice obsolete. The sacrifices pointed to Him making the law unnecessary for salvation.

As Jesus said, flee to the mountains when this destruction happens. The Jewish population in Jerusalem was almost down to zero until a buildup encouraged by the British occurred around 1827.

Here are signs of the times given in the <u>Jewish Voice Today</u> publication. (3rd quarter 2017)

1. A restored Israel and Jewish Jerusalem where Jesus will return
   - Israel rebirthed in a Day – May 14, 1948
   - Jerusalem Restored into Jewish Hands – June 1967 per six Day War
   - The Desert will bloom and blossoms. Israel is producing lush crops
   - Hebrew language revived – In late 1800's Russian immigrants to Israel, Eliezer Ben-Yehudah, revived the ancient Hebrew language, giving the returning exiles of Israel a common language.

2. Israel surrounded by conflict and the rise of antisemitism.
3. The regathering of the Jewish people physically back to the land of Israel from the four corners of the earth. Deuteronomy 30-34, Isaiah 11:11-12, Jeremiah 16:14-15
4. The Gospel is proclaimed to the nations
5. The blindness being removed from the eyes of the Jewish people.

The signs given here from a Jewish perspective are dramatic and clear. This is what the Sovereign Lord says: I will take the Israelites out of the nations where they have gone. I will gather them from all around and bring them back into their own land. I will make them one nation in the land, on the mountain of Israel. Ezekiel 37:21-22. Another sign is the return of the people of Israel to their land. In 1948 the State of Israel formally declared its independence which was recognized by the United States and several other countries. In 2018 Israel celebrated its 70th anniversary. This is what God promised to them.

Today on television, I witnessed the celebration of the United States opening its embassy in Jerusalem, a sign of Jesus soon return. Soon, Jerusalem will be the Capital of Israel again. What a historic event! It's significance, importance, and excitement are because of when it is a sign. Deuteronomy 30:34, Isaiah 11:12 and Jeremiah 16:15, bring promises of God, speak to the final existence of Jewish Israel in this world. In Isaiah 2:2-5 God says "In the last days – the law will go out from Zion the word of the Lord from Jerusalem. Now we must ask God to bring peace to that area so they and their neighbors will have full access to the Gospel of Jesus Christ of Bethlehem and Heaven.

Here is an informative paragraph from a monthly letter from Jews for Jesus. It emphasizes the importance of Jerusalem and an event that will happen soon.

"Isaiah assures us that ultimately God will rejoice over Jerusalem the way a groom rejoices over his bride." "Because you love the Word of God and the purposes of God, I ask you to join us in praying for the peace of Jerusalem-and for our upcoming outreach there."

During the last 130 years Jews from 108 nations have migrated to the land of Israel. The Nazis killings of around 6 million Jews made it clear to the Jews that they needed a homeland. Today Israel's population is over 7 million. This small country is surrounded by hostile countries that vow to destroy her. Yet they cannot! Anti-Jewish sentiment is increasing as the time of Jesus return comes closer. Satan will not be able to do this until the last day. Jesus said they will be hated by all nations because of me. Matthew 24:9.

Christian Headlines reported that Vice President Mike Pence warned world leaders of an Iranian plot for another Holocaust in Israel. He continued noting remarks made by the former Supreme Leader of Iran. Pence said, "Ayotollah Khomeini himself said that it is the mission of the Islamic Republic of Iran to erase Israel from the map." The Iranian regime openly advocates another Holocaust and it seeks the means to achieve it," Pence warned. "Anti-Semitism must be confronted wherever and whenever it arises, Pence said, and it must be universally condemned."

Regarding point #5 with the blindness being removed from the eyes of the Jewish people, God has created many organizations for use by the Holy Spirit. Jeremiah 31:31-34 speaks of the new covenant with the house of Israel and is quoted again in Hebrew 8:10. Here God is talking of the "last days" or the fulness of the Jewish people when they will know Jesus as their Savior, the promised Messiah! This occurs at the same time as the "fulness of the Gentiles"! He says "you people will all know me" and "I will remember their sins no more". I counted 75 Messianic Groups in Israel and many more in the United States that work for that purpose. They are supported by workers, by prayers and by financial support. Surely this is our God preparing His people for Jesus return. This is why the nations hate the Jews and us.

Two essential symptomatic events that corresponds with the graphs increasing rapid upward movement to final culmination is given in Romans 11:25-26. "Israel has experienced a hardening in part until the full number of Gentiles has come in." One is the way of salvation in Jesus alone, the Word of God, is almost in every language for the occurrence of fulness of the Gentiles.

The second is seen from the growing numbers of Messianic Jews, the supporting organizations God is using to soften the hearts to receive Him, the return of His people from all over the world from where they were scattered, and the miraculous protection of Israel's existence in the face of surrounding hostile nations, is evidence of the soon fulfillment of the Jews.

Another sign I believe is relevant is the extraordinary progress (blessings) made by the nations as compared to all of history. From BC1 there was basically minimal change as to the ease of life. As evidence that the lack of change affects some people's faith, in 2 Peter 3:4 scoffers said." "Where is this "coming" He promised? Ever since our fathers died, everything goes on as it has since the beginning of creation." Distance, communication, transportation, medical advancement, food production, and technology and many other advancements speak of a dramatic, radical change in history in a short period of time. Most of this occurred in the last 50 years.

In many countries there is ample food, a variety all year long, sanitation, unprecedented health care, indoor plumbing, and extended life expectancy. I believe the life expectancy of the American Indian was 35 years. My grandfather died from a "simple ailment" that could have readily been prevented in the last 50 years. I could go on pointing out the amazing blessings we have today given in a very short span of time.

In lets say, 6000 plus years of human history, the greatest notable change was in the last 60 years giving a time ratio of 1/100. So in the last 1% of all the days since Adam fell (he could have lived in Eden a million years before he fell into sin as he did not count days or years because there was no death at that time) I would give a change ratio of 100/1, or 100 times extraordinary advancement in quality of life as far as available opportunity and ease of life in an incredibly short time.

What is the point I am trying to make with this change in history? I believe that the sudden change is a sign that Jesus is returning soon. Projecting the increase in technology and man's negative use of that and other sinful behavior on a global scale, it is easy to see worldwide disaster in the near future. Therefore, our passion and work must be urgent in action to get the fact of His soon return to all people. Time is short!

Recently, in the news, was a report on a workplace activity that was somewhat frightening. There was a company that was inserting a "chip" under the skin of the hand of employees that would give them clearance at their work. Could this be a precursor given in Revelation 13:16-17? That is the prediction of the mark on the right hand or the forehead, so no one can buy or sell unless he has the mark, that is, the name of the beast or the number of his name. That number is 666.

Since we live on this side of the cross one of the most wonderful advancements in history is the printing press and the radio that have enabled us to flood the world with the Scripture.

For all the given signs, I believe the graph offers the only accurate time of Jesus's return.

CHAPTER 5

To God's Chosen People – The Jews

We, as Gentiles, owe the life-giving Scriptures to the Jewish people, for God, made them responsible for the message of salvation to all peoples. Isaiah 49:6 says "I will make you, the Jews, a light for the Gentiles, that you may bring my salvation to the ends of the earth". Our Jesus from the tribe of Judah says in John 4:22, "that salvation is from the Jews."

This chapter is dedicated to you dear people with the hope that many of you will see that the Old Testament Prophecies of the Messiah are all fulfilled in the New Testament. Our Jewish Savior loves His people dearly. He wants you to know Him and love Him.

I pray that this chapter will clearly show that the One first revealed in the Pentuchute, in the Old Testament, is the promised Messiah whom many of you still seek and is revealed in the New Testament. It was the Jewish apostles and Paul who were called by God to begin the work of the Great Commission, bringing the Gospel throughout the world to the Gentiles. Paul says in Philippians 3:5 that he was circumcised on the eighth day of the people of Israel, of the Tribe of Benjamin, a Hebrew of Hebrews, in regard to the law, a Pharisee – as for persecuting the way, as for legalistic righteous, faultless. Paul was destroying the church. Until, on the way to Damascus with a letter from the high priest in Jerusalem to destroy the Way he had a vision of Jesus. Jesus asked why he was persecuting Him. After Paul's conversation, he says" the Gospel is the power of salvation to everyone who believes to the Jews first and also to the Gentiles". He who was a pure Jew, along with the Jewish disciples began the spread of the Word to the Jews and Gentiles with the power of the Holy Spirit. So, we Gentiles must say, thank you dear Jewish people. We will continue to show our gratitude to you in Heaven!

After Jesus resurrection, Luke in Chapter 24, gives the account of His meeting two men on the way to Emaus who were downcast because of the death of Jesus of Nazareth. <u>²⁵He said to them, "How foolish you are, and how slow to believe all that the prophets have spoken! ²⁶Did not the Messiah have to suffer these things and then enter his glory?" ²⁷And beginning with Moses and all the Prophets, he explained to them what was said in all the Scriptures concerning himself. (Luke 24:25-27).</u>

To this day, those from the "tribe of Judah" hold to the Pentuchute of Moses as written by Jahweh. They also believe the historical accounts of the prophets and many of the Psalms have been written by their notable ruler – King David. In this chapter of Luke, Jesus is saying – look, Moses, the Prophets and the Psalms speak of me. The promised Messiah has come for this first time as was predicted. He then proceeds to substantiate His claim with the gospel "according to the Old Testament."

It is well known to the Reformed Faith that God's plan of salvation is in every book in the Old Testament. The writing would serve no purpose apart from this fact.

The axiom, the New is in the Old contained, the Old is by the New explained neatly explains this fact.

One intent of this writing is to erase the division of the Testaments and show it is one book, not two. This is done using the irresistible, convincing authority of the writing of the Holy Spirit paralleling them (the writings) in an attempt to convince first the Jews and then the Gentile that the first coming of Christ is a fact of history, and now all must prepare for His second coming which is not too far distant.

Jesus tells His disciples in Luke 24:44 "This is what I told you while I was still with you: Everything must be fulfilled that is written about me in the Law of Moses, the Prophets, and the Psalms.

Many Jewish people are followers of Christ today. Along with them I plead with those who are not, will do what He said in Luke 24 and believe on His name by the Power of the Holy Spirit.

Because of Israel's, disobedience, they were scattered through distant lands as reported in Deuteronomy 30 and other Old Testament Scripture. God promised to bring them back to the promised land. In Deuteronomy 30:1-5 God tells extensively of the Jews return which is clearly what is happening today, beginning in earnest in 1948 when Israel became a nation. Nehemiah repeats this promise in this prayer." He will bring them back to the place He has chosen as a dwelling for my Name (Nehemiah 1:8-9). This return of Israel is of historical proportion and is clearly visible today. The elucidation of this paragraph is found in Chapter 3 where it covers the recognition of Jerusalem as Israel's capital and in Chapter 4 as one of the signs of Jesus second coming.

Hopefully the following parallism of the Old Testament / New Testament will be convincing.

Here are the two texts that summarize the complete revelation to man from our God.

Psalm 103:11-12

[11] For as high as the heavens are above the earth, so great is his love for those who fear him; [12] as far as the east is from the west, so far has he removed our transgressions from us.

John 3:16

[16] For God so loved the world that he gave his one and only Son, that whoever believes in him shall not perish but have eternal life.

There are more than 300 scripture verses (prophesies) in the Old Testament that speak of Jesus. He Himself quoted many of them to fulfill and to teach. Please read Luke 4:16-21e what He taught on the Sabbath day in the synagogue.

Jesus said to His disciples "this is what I told you, everything must be fulfilled that is written about me in the law of Moses the Prophets and the Psalms". (Luke 24:44)

As recorded in John 5:46-47, The Jewish church officials were troubling Jeshua as He healed on the Sabbath day. He told the Jewish authorities that their accuser is Moses on whom they set their hope and that if they believed Moses, they would believe Him as Moses writes about Jeshua.

In 1 Corinthians 15:3-9, Paul says "For what I received I passed on to you as of first importance: that Christ died for our sins according to the Scriptures, that he was buried, that he was raised on the third day according to the Scriptures, and that he appeared to Peter, and then to the Twelve. After that he appeared to more than five hundred of the brothers at the same time, most of whom are still living, though some have fallen asleep. Then he appeared to James, then to all the apostles, and last of all he appeared to me also, as to one abnormally born.

For I am the least of the apostles and do not even deserve to be called an apostle, because I persecuted the church of God. But by the grace of God I am what I am, and his grace to me was not without effect.

Paul makes certain that what he is saying is according to the Scriptures.

Here are some of the parallel Old Testament / New Testament prophecy fulfillment, the interpretative and explanation of the entire Bible. To keep this as "cookies on the lower shelf" for rapid reading, and to keep one's interest, the number of quotations from Scripture here are limited.

Genesis 3:15

And I will put enmity between you and the woman, and between your offspring[a] and hers; he will crush[b] your head, and you will strike his heel."

Revelation 12:17

Then the dragon was enraged at the woman and went off to wage war against the rest of her offspring— those who keep God's commands and hold fast their testimony about Jesus.

Exodus 3:14

God said to Moses, "I AM WHO I AM.[a] This is what you are to say to the Israelites: 'I AM has sent me to you.'"

John 8:58

Very truly I tell you," Jesus answered, "before Abraham was born, I am!"

Deuteronomy 6:5

5 Love the LORD your God with all your heart and with all your soul and with all your strength.

Matthew 22:36-40

36 "Teacher, which is the greatest commandment in the Law?"
37 Jesus replied: "'Love the Lord your God with all your heart and with all your soul and with all your mind.'[a]

Deuteronomy 10:17

For the LORD your God is God of gods and Lord of lords, the great God, mighty and awesome, who shows no partiality and accepts no bribes.

Revelation 19:16

On his robe and on his thigh, he has this name written:

KING OF KINGS AND LORD OF LORDS.

Deuteronomy 18:15

The LORD your God will raise up for you a prophet like me from among you, from your fellow Israelites. You must listen to him.

John 5:46

If you believed Moses, you would believe me, for he wrote about me.

Deuteronomy 18:15

The LORD your God will raise up for you a prophet like me from among you, from your fellow Israelites. You must listen to him.

Acts 3:22

For Moses said, 'The Lord your God will raise up for you a prophet like me from among your own people; you must listen to everything he tells you

Deuteronomy 21:22-23

22 If someone guilty of a capital offense is put to death
    and their body is exposed on a pole,
23 you must not leave the body hanging on the pole overnight.

    Be sure to bury it that same day, because anyone who is hung on a pole is under God's curse.

    You must not desecrate the land the LORD your God
    is giving you as an inheritance.

Acts 5:30-31

30 The God of our fathers raised up Jesus, whom ye slew and hanged on a tree.
31 Him hath God exalted with his right hand to be a Prince and a Savior, for to give repentance to Israel, and forgiveness of sins.

I Samuel 16:1

1The Lord said to Samuel, "How long will you go on grieving over Saul? I have rejected him as king of Israel.

    But now get some olive oil and go to Bethlehem, to a man named Jesse, because I have chosen one of his
    sons to be king."

Romans 1:3

3It is about his Son, our Lord Jesus Christ: as to his humanity, he was born a descendant of David;

Psalm 2:7

I will proclaim the LORD's decree:
He said to me, "You are my son;
    today I have become your father.

Hebrews 5:5

In the same way, Christ did not take on himself the glory of becoming a high priest. But God said to him, "You are my Son; today I have become your Father."

Psalm 22:1

1 My God, my God, why have you forsaken me?

Matthew 27:46

46 About three in the afternoon Jesus cried out in a loud voice, *"Eli, Eli lema sabachthani?"*(which means "My God, my God, why have you forsaken me?").[b]

Psalm 22:7

[7] All who see me mock me; they hurl <u>insults</u>, shaking their heads.

Mark 15:29

[29] Those who passed by hurled <u>insults</u> at him, shaking their heads and saying, "So! You who are going to destroy the temple and build it in three days,

Psalm 22:18

[18] They divide my clothes among them and cast lots for my garment.

Matthew 27:28 & 31

[28] They stripped him and put a scarlet robe on him,
[31] After they had mocked him, they took off the robe and put his own clothes on him. Then they led him away to crucify him.

Psalm 69:21

[21] They put gall in my food and gave me vinegar for my thirst.

Mark 15:36

[36] Someone ran, filled a sponge with <u>wine vinegar</u>, put it on a staff, and <u>offered</u> it to Jesus to drink. "Now leave him alone. Let's see if Elijah comes to take him down," he said.

Psalm 78:2

[2] I will open my mouth with a parable; I will utter hidden things, things from of old—

Matthew 13:34-35

[34] Jesus spoke all these things to the crowd in parables; he did not say anything to them without using a parable.
[35] So was fulfilled what was spoken through the prophet: "I will open my mouth in parables, I will utter things hidden since the creation of the world."[a]

Psalm 118:22-23

[22] The stone the builders rejected has become the cornerstone;
[23] the LORD has done this, and it is marvelous in our eyes.

Mark 12:10

[10] Haven't you read this passage of Scripture: "'The stone the builders rejected has become the cornerstone;

Ezekiel 37:10

My dwelling place will be with them; I will be their God, and they will be my people.

Revelation 21:3

And I heard a loud voice from the throne saying, "Look! God's dwelling place is now among the people, and he will dwell with them. They will be his people, and God himself will be with them and be their God.

Daniel 7:14 & Zechariah 14:9

He was given authority, glory and sovereign power; all nations and peoples of every language worshiped him. His dominion is an everlasting dominion that will not pass away, and his kingdom is one that will never be destroyed.

The LORD will be king over the whole earth. On that day there will be one LORD, and his name the only name.

Revelation 11:15

The seventh angel sounded his trumpet, and there were loud voices in heaven, which said:
"The kingdom of the world has become the kingdom of our Lord and of his Messiah, and he will reign for ever and ever."

Matthew Chapter 1 gives a record of the genealogy of Jesus Christ, the Son of David, the Son of Abraham.

Verse 2 - Abraham was the father of Isaac
Isaac was the father of Jacob
Jacob was the father of Judah

Verse 6 – Jesse was the father of King David
David was the father of Solomon

Verse 15 – Eliad the father of Eleazar
Eleazar the father of Mattham
Matthem the father of Jacob

Verse 16 – and Jacob the father of Joseph the husband of Mary, of whom was born Jesus, who is called Christ (Messiah).

Verse 17 – Then there were fourteen generations in all from Abraham to David, fourteen from David to the exile to Babylon, and fourteen from exile to Jesus, the Christ.

I urge you, the people of the God of the Old Testament, to read this genealogy of your family. You will meet all of them in the New Jerusalem!

Hosea 11:1

"When Israel was a child, I loved him, and out of Egypt I called my son."

Matthew 2:15

[15] where he stayed until the death of Herod. and so was fulfilled what the Lord had said through the prophet: "Out of Egypt I called my son."[a]

Isaiah 7:14

Therefore the Lord himself will give you[a] a sign: The virgin[b] will conceive and give birth to a son, and[c] will call him Immanuel.

Luke 1:29-31

[29] Mary was greatly troubled at his words and wondered what kind of greeting this might be. [30] But the angel said to her, "Do not be afraid, Mary; you have found favor with God. [31] You will conceive and give birth to a son, and you are to call him Jesus

Isaiah 9:7

Of the greatness of his government and peace there will be no end. He will reign on David's throne and over his kingdom, establishing and upholding it with justice and righteousness from that time on and forever. The zeal of the LORD Almighty will accomplish this.

Luke 1:32-33

[32] He will be great and will be called the Son of the Most High. The Lord God will give him the throne of his father David, [33] and he will reign over Jacob's descendants forever; his kingdom will never end."

Isaiah 11:1

A shoot will come up from the stump of Jesse; from his roots a Branch will bear fruit.

Romans 15:12

and again, Isaiah says, "The Root of Jesse will spring up, one who will arise to rule over the nations; in him the Gentiles will hope."[a]

Revelations 22:16

"I, Jesus, have sent my angel to give you[a] this testimony for the churches. I am the Root and the Offspring of David, and the bright Morning Star."

Isaiah 28:16

So this is what the Sovereign LORD says:

"See, I lay a stone in Zion, a tested stone, a precious cornerstone for a sure foundation; the one who relies on it will never be stricken with panic.

Acts 4:12

Jesus is "'the stone you builders rejected, which has become the cornerstone.'[a]
[12] Salvation is found in no one else, for there is no other name under heaven given to mankind by which we must be saved."

Isaiah 53:5

But he was pierced for our transgressions, he was crushed for our iniquities; the punishment that brought us peace was on him, and by his wounds we are healed.

I Corinthians 15:3

For what I received I passed on to you as of first importance[a]: that Christ died for our sins according to the Scriptures,

Isaiah 44:6

"This is what the LORD says Israel's King and Redeemer, the LORD Almighty:
I am the first and I am the last; apart from me there is no God.

Revelation 22:13

I am the Alpha and the Omega, the First and the Last, the Beginning and the End.

Isaiah 53:5

But he was pierced for our transgressions, he was crushed for our iniquities; the punishment that brought us peace was on him, and by his wounds we are healed.

I Peter 2:24

He himself bore our sins" in his body on the cross, so that we might die to sins and live for righteousness; "by his wounds you have been healed."

Isaiah 53:7

[7] He was oppressed and afflicted, yet he did not open his mouth; he was led like a lamb to the slaughter, and as a sheep before its shearers is silent, so he did not open his mouth.

Mark 14:61

[61] But Jesus remained silent and gave no answer. Again the high priest asked him, "Are you the Messiah, the Son of the Blessed One?"

Micah 5:2

"But you, Bethlehem Ephrathah, though you are small among the clans[a] of Judah,out of you will come for me one who will be ruler over Israel, whose origins are from of old, from ancient times."

John 7:41-42

Others said, "He is the Messiah."Still others asked, "How can the Messiah come from Galilee? [42] Does not Scripture say that the Messiah will come from David's descendants and from Bethlehem, the town where David lived?"

Matthew 2:1

After Jesus was born in Bethlehem in Judea, during the time of King Herod, Magi[a] from the east came to Jerusalem

Zechariah 9:9

Rejoice greatly, Daughter Zion! Shout, Daughter Jerusalem! See, your king comes to you, righteous and victorious, lowly and riding on a donkey, on a colt, the foal of a donkey.

John 12:14-16

Jesus found a young donkey and sat on it, as it is written Do not be afraid, Daughter Zion; see, your king is coming, seated on a donkey's colt."[a]

[16] At first his disciples did not understand all this. Only after Jesus was glorified did they realize that these things had been written about him and that these things had been done to him.

Zechariah 12:10

And I will pour out on the house of David and the inhabitants of Jerusalem a spirit[a] of grace and supplication. They will look on[b] me, the one they have pierced, and they will mourn for him as one mourns for an only child, and grieve bitterly for him as one grieves for a firstborn son.

John 19:33-37

But when they came to Jesus and found that he was already dead, they did not break his legs. [34] Instead, one of the soldiers pierced Jesus' side with a spear, bringing a sudden flow of blood and water.

[36] These things happened so that the scripture would be fulfilled: "Not one of his bones will be broken,"[a]

[37] and, as another scripture says, "They will look on the one they have pierced."

Zechariah 13:7

[7] "Awake, sword, against my shepherd, against the man who is close to me!" declares the LORD Almighty. "Strike the shepherd, and the sheep will be scattered, and I will turn my hand against the little ones.

Matthew 26:31-32

[31] Then Jesus told them, "This very night you will all fall away on account of me, for it is written: "'I will strike the shepherd, and the sheep of the flock will be scattered.'[a]

[32] But after I have risen, I will go ahead of you into Galilee."

Isaiah 49:6 .... Acts 13:47

he says: | For this is what the Lord has commanded us: "'I have
"It is too small a thing for you to be my servant to | made you[a] a light for the Gentiles, that you[b] may
restore the tribes of Jacob and bring back those of | bring salvation to the ends of the earth.'[c]"
Israel I have kept. I will also make you a light for the
Gentiles, that my salvation may reach to the ends of
the earth."

> Our Jewish brothers and sisters in Christ. Look what God has said, He will do and has done for
> us Gentiles using you. You are a very special people to us! "Salvation to the ends of the earth"
> is what Jesus told us in Matthew 24:14 "and this Gospel of the Kingdom will be preached in
> the whole world as a testimony to all nations, and then the end will come".

Luke 2:25-32 25 Now there was a man in Jerusalem called Simeon, who was righteous and devout. He was waiting for the consolation of Israel, and the Holy Spirit was on him. 26 It had been revealed to him by the Holy Spirit that he would not die before he had seen the Lord's Messiah. 27 Moved by the Spirit, he went into the temple courts. When the parents brought in the child Jesus to do for him what the custom of the Law required, 28 Simeon took him in his arms and praised God, saying:29 "Sovereign Lord, as you have promised, you may now dismiss[a] your servant in peace.30 For my eyes have seen your salvation,31 which you have prepared in the sight of all nations:32 a light for revelation to the Gentiles, and the glory of your people Israel.

After Jesus sacrifice, resurrection, and return to Heaven, the Holy Temple was destroyed which ended animal sacrifice. The blood of animals did not and cannot pay for man's sins. The practice began after Adam's fall and pointed to the ultimate sacrifice of God's Son. When He was on the cross and said "it is finished" the curtain of the Temple that separated the Holy Place from the Most Holy Place was torn from top to bottom. This ended the demands of the old law, ended sacrifices and replaced them with the Love of God that paid for all the sins of His people, including back to Adam and Eve. This is why there will be no more animal sacrifices for sins as the debt was paid in full at approximately 33 AD. (Read Hebrews 10:3-12)

As I understand these Samaritans that Jesus spent time with in John 4, had only the first five (5) books of the Bible. Yet when Jesus spent time at Jacobs well in Samaria with a Samaritan woman, and she is perceiving that He was a prophet said to Him in John 4:25 "I know that Messiah (called Christ) is coming. When He comes He will explain everything to us". She got this from Deuteronomy 18:15. "The Lord your God will raise up for you a prophet like me from among your own brothers. You must listen to Him. This is repeated in verse 18 and in Acts 3:22. Jesus said to her "I who speak to you am He." So the promised Messiah is found in Genesis, Exodus, Leviticus, Numbers, and Deuteronomy. After Jesus spent two days in Samaria and explained how the Pentateuch pointed to Him, they believed He is the promised Messiah. Jewish tradition refers to this collection as the Book of the Law or the Law and the Torah.

In Mark 10:47, there is the healing of blind Bartimaeus (son of Timaeus). When he heard that it was Jesus of Nazareth walking by, he began to shout "Jesus, Son of David, have mercy on me!" He could not see Jesus before He healed his eyes, but knew He was the Son of David. This was a popular Title for the coming Messiah in that day and often used when Jesus healed someone.

Some other events that pointed to Jesus.

In Numbers 21:8 Moses made a bronze snake and put it on a pole. All who were bitten by a venomous snake and looked at the pole were healed. In John 3:14-15 Jesus said "Just as Moses lifted up the snake in the wilderness, so the Son of Man must be lifted up,[a] 15 that everyone who believes may have eternal life in him."

Abraham was about to sacrifice his ONLY SON on an altar, but God stopped him. It was a test for Abraham but really pointed to Christ, Gods ONLY SON. Isaac willingly carried the wood; Jesus willingly carried the wooden cross. It must have been very painful for Abraham. It was indescribable, infinite pain for Jesus Father to see His Son sacrificed and had to forsake Him to save us. Jesus said, "it is finished" and died at 3 PM when the shofor was blown from the animal sacrifice, possibly the same time of day as Isaac was laid on the altar.

The Passover used blood on the door post and unleavened bread. "The Lords Supper" in Matthew 26, unleavened bread representing His body as the Passover Lamb, and wine, representing His blood was the beginning of this faith strengthening sacrament. This will also be the first event in Heaven when all of us gather with Jesus at the Wedding Feast.

Exodus 3:14 God told Moses to tell the Israelites that the "I Am" sent me.

John 8:58 Jesus said" before Abraham was, "I Am" No beginning or end

The seven (7) feasts given in Leviticus 23 all point to Jesus.

- Passover Feast 23:5 – also in Genesis 14:18 Melchizedek brought bread and wine to Abraham-same day as Jesus "Last Supper" on Good Friday.
- Unleavened Bread 23:6
- First Fruits 23:11
- Pentecost 23:8 – 50 days – Holy Spirit poured out 50 days after Jesus's resurrection.
- Trumpets 23:24
- Days of atonement 23:27 – Jesus paid it all
- Feast of Tabernacles 23:34

Dear Jewish people, the family where our Savior is from, the God who loves you with an infinite love, stands waiting for you to seek Him. He is grieving, like in the Old Testament, as you reject Him. He is appealing to you, no, He is pleading with you to search the Scriptures and find Him, God the Father, God the Son, and God the Holy Spirit. After Jesus triumphant entry into Jerusalem predicted in Zechariah 9:9 riding on a foal of a donkey, Luke says in chapter 19:41 "As he approached Jerusalem and saw the city, He wept over it. Please read this account and feel His grief for you His people!"

Please come my Jewish Brothers in Christ. He will not return until you do, according to the Scriptures. I am asking the Holy Spirit to make the Scriptures plain to you, to every descendant of Abraham, Isaac, and Jacob living today!

The hope for many Jews today is still the rescue by a Messiah from their enemies once and for all. They are expecting God to set up a permanent "kingdom" on this planet for them. In addition, they want to rebuild the temple and once again offer animal sacrifices as given in Old Testament law. Hosea 6:6 says "For I desire mercy , not sacrifice, and acknowledgment (love) of God, rather than burnt offerings." God has promised and will indeed defeat all enemies of the Jews, including sin and death. This will not result in an earthly kingdom but a heavenly one. The promised Messiah will do this and He will be (and is) the ruler over all the universe. What He has prepared for you His people, is indescribably wonderful!

The King to rescue Israel is the Messiah described in Isaiah 53. This is the One that the Jews are looking for today, not them only, but the Gentiles as well. Israel did not crown kings but <u>anointed them</u> as reference to the kings relationship to God. Isaiah 61:1 says "The Spirit of the Sovereign Lord is in me, because <u>the Lord has anointed me</u> to preach good news to the poor". Acts 10:38 says <u>"how God anointed Jesus of Nazareth with the Holy Spirit</u> and power and how He went around doing good and healing".

It was man's fallen nature to worship visible objects, so God gave laws and commandments to have no other Gods before Him and no graven images or heavenly deities as gods to honor. Image worship was a temptation presented by the surrounding nations, so God wanted to keep them separate and not copy pagan worship. We have been as guilty as the Israelites in falling into that trap!

The animal sacrifices pointed to Jesus and they saved no one. *Isaiah 40:16 says "all of Lebanon's forest do not contain sufficient fuel to consume a sacrifice large enough to honor Him. All Lebanon's sacrificial animals would not make an offering worthy of our God" *New Living Translation – Reference Edition The faith of Abraham, Isaac, and Jacob and their following of the law did not save them. Their hope was in the coming Savior, Jeshua, promised to them and the whole world. It was, and is, only the blood sacrifice of Jeshua that saved them and saves us. This once and for all sacrifice saves all His people from Adam to the last believer in Him at His return. The blood on the doorpost, the final plague on the Egyptians, pointed to this saving blood. The apostle Paul writes, addressing this in Galatians 3:24-25, "so the law was our guardian until Christ came that we might be justified by faith. Now that this faith has come, we are no longer under a guardian."

The renting of veil in the Temple from top to bottom separated the Holy Place from the Holy of Holies opening a new and living way into the presence of God through His death on the cross. This negated animal sacrifices (Hebrews 10:4) and keeping of the law as saving works. We no longer need laws and priests in the temple between us and our loving God the Father (Hebrews 10:11-12). We now go to Him directly through our great High Priest, Jesus Christ, who fulfilled the law and paid the penalty of our sins. Jesus says in John 14:6, "I am <u>the</u> way, <u>the</u> truth and <u>the</u> life. No one comes to the Father except through me." Now we go to Him through Jesus with our love, praises, and requests. In Galatians 3:24 Paul says "let me put it another way. The law was our guardian and teacher to lead us until Christ came. So now, through faith in Christ, we are made right with God."

Surely, this tearing of the veil to God's dwelling place with the Jews (Shekinah glory) is recorded somewhere in Jewish history of the Temple. This occurred when Jesus died on the cross and said, "It is Finished"! (Matthew 27:51)

A clear example that we are not saved by works or keeping the law is seen by what happened to the one thief on the cross. He did not have any good works to bring or keeping of the Old Testament laws. Nor did he believe in Jeshua until hanging on the cross with Him. Yet, Jesus took him to paradise because he finally believed, and all his sins were washed away like our sins, by Jesus blood shed on the cross. He told the thief, who admitted his being crucified was justified, "today you will be with me in Paradise."

There are numerous, Messianic organizations in Israel to help you in your spiritual faith, education, help for orphans, widows, broken hearts, and those in poverty.

Here are some of the 75 Messianic organizations in Israel.
Aviv-Ministry – Social ministry in Tel-Aviv.
Bert Ha Yeshua – Bring Jewish people back to Israel

Come to Zion – Hebrew Roots study.
First Fruits of Zion – Study of Scriptures, historical, cultural, linguistics

Hope for Israel – Bring hope of Messiah back to Israel

Intercessors for Israel – Prayers for Israel

International Fellowship of Christians and Jews – Helping the impoverished

Jewish Voice Ministries – Humanitarian Aid

Jews for Jesus – Missionary Team

Kah-Katuv – Bible Studies

Messiah's Mandate – Leaders for coming Israel revival

Messianic Jewish Bible Institute – establish Jewish congregation

Netivah – Youth Ministry

One for Israel – Ways to bless Israel

Ot OoMofet Ministries – In-reach to orphans and widows

Redeemed in Zion – Social Assistance

The Joseph Project – Helping those in poverty

Trumpet of Salvation to Israel – Good Tidings to Israel

Yetzeron – Educational Publishing for Youth

Zions Glory – Ahavat Yeshua Messianic Congregation in Jerusalem

The number of Messianic Jews and their organizations is so encouraging to me as I believe this is another fulfillment of the "signs of the times" given in Jeremiah 31:31. Here God says "the time is coming declares the Lord, when I will make a new covenant with the house of Israel. In Hebrews 8:8 He says "The time is coming, declares the Lord, when I will make a new covenant with the house of Judah". Verse 34 of Jeremiah 31 and Hebrews 8:11 He says "No longer will a man teach his neighbor or a man his brother saying "know the Lord" because they will all know me from the least of them to the greatest". Why does Jeshua say this? The reason is found in Jeremiah 31:3. "I have loved you, Israel, with an everlasting love, I have drawn you with loving – kindness." So not only the sign of returning Israel to their land but the promise of the new covenant is now here namely, Jesus!

The "softening" of the Jewish heart, the acceptance of Jeshua, is evidenced by the many Messianic Jews. Romans 11:25 says "Israel has experienced a hardening in part" until the full number of the Gentiles has come in! Then in verse 26 "and all Israel will be saved". This is because" I will put my laws in their minds and write them on their hearts". (Hebrews 8:10, Jeremiah 31) So then God says in Isaiah 59:20 "The Redeemer will come to Zion to those in Jacob who repent of their sins."

This now puts a responsibility on you, my Jewish brethren in Christ. In Isaiah 49:6 Jehovah says, "I will also make you a light for the Gentiles that you may bring my salvation to the ends of the earth." He is talking about the simultaneous fulness of the Jews and fulness of the Gentiles. We must all work together to complete this and bring Him back. In Romans 10:12 God says "For there is no difference between Jew and Gentile the same Lord is Lord of all and richly blesses all who call on Him, for everyone who calls on the name of the Lord will be saved." Romans 1:16 says: For I am not ashamed of the gospel, because it is the power of God that brings salvation to everyone who believes: first to the Jew, then to the Gentile.

The New Testament book of Hebrews was written to the Jews. I urge you dear people to read this spiritual and historical exposition of the Old Testament laws. Here is a little annotation from an NIV Study Bible.

Date
Hebrews must have been written before the destruction of Jerusalem and the temple in A.D. 70 because: (1) had it been written after this date, the author surely would have mentioned the temple's destruction and the end of the Jewish sacrificial system; and (2) the author consistently uses the Greek present tense when speaking of the temple and the priestly activities connected with it.

Recipients
The letter was addressed primarily to Jewish converts who were familiar with the OT and who were being tempted to revert to Judaism or to Judaize the gospel (cf Gal 2:14). Some have suggested that these professing Jewish Christians were thinking of merging with a Jewish sect, such as the one at Qumran near the Dead Sea. It has also been suggested that the recipients were from the "large number of priests who became obedient to the faith" (Ac 6:7)

I appeal to all Jewish people around the world, my brothers and sisters in Christ to help bring Jeshua back as He promised to do. <u>He will not return until you accept Him as the Messiah you were looking for since your Father Abraham.</u> Would you not want to meet him along with Isaac, Jacob, Moses, Elijah, Joshua and all the prophets of Jehovah? You could meet and spend time with each one in heaven. We Gentiles are looking forward to meeting them plus all those we know from the Scriptures like Noah, David, Adam & Eve, et al. (Hope there is a New International Version in Heaven.) Time will not be limited.

The <u>Jewish Voice Today</u> magazine of 3rd Quarter 2018 makes the following statement. "Yeshua will not return until the Jewish leadership in Jerusalem recognizes Him as Messiah."

Thank you so much for being a light of salvation to us Gentiles. We will forever be indebted and thankful to you. In John 4:22 Jesus says "salvation is from the Jews!"

"Salvation is found in no one else, for there is no other name given under heaven to man by which we must be saved" – than the Jewish Jesus. (Acts 4:12)

Holy Spirit, in Jeshua's name, please make the Scriptures you wrote plain to every descendant of Abraham, Isaac, and Jacob living today and until He returns. Please repeat what you did in Jerusalem at the Feast of Weeks, First Fruits, Harvest or Pentecost, given in Acts 2, for every Jew around the world.

In Isaiah 49:6 and Acts 13:47 God says" This is what the lord has commanded us. "I have made you a light for the Gentiles that you may bring salvation to the ends of the earth". Ephesians 2:19 "You (Gentiles) are no longer foreigners and aliens, but fellow citizens with God's people (Jews) and members of God's household, built on the foundation of the apostles and prophets with Christ Jesus Himself as the chief cornerstone."

In Acts chapter 7, Stephen was appointed a deacon by the apostles in Jerusalem. He was filled with the Holy Spirit and taught the Word of God. Members of the Synagogue produced false witnesses saying he blasphemed God and Moses. He had to appear before the Sanhedrin and his defense is in large part a review of Jewish biblical history linking the old testament messianic promises fulfilled at that time.

Acts 7 New International Version (NIV)

Stephen's Speech to the Sanhedrin

Acts 7:1 Then the high priest asked Stephen, "Are these charges true?"

[2] To this he replied: "Brothers and fathers, listen to me! The God of glory appeared to our father Abraham while he was still in Mesopotamia, before he lived in Harran. [3] 'Leave your country and your people,' God said, 'and go to the land I will show you.'[a]

[4] "So he left the land of the Chaldeans and settled in Harran. After the death of his father, God sent him to this land where you are now living. [5] He gave him no inheritance here, not even enough ground to set his foot on. But God promised him that he and his descendants after him would possess the land, even though at that time Abraham had no child. [6] God spoke to him in this way: 'For four hundred years your descendants will be strangers in a country not their own, and they will be enslaved and mistreated. [7] But I will punish the nation they serve as slaves,' God said, 'and afterward they will come out of that country and worship me in this place.'[b] [8] Then he gave Abraham the covenant of circumcision. And Abraham became the father of Isaac and circumcised him eight days after his birth. Later Isaac became the father of Jacob, and Jacob became the father of the twelve patriarchs.

[9] "Because the patriarchs were jealous of Joseph, they sold him as a slave into Egypt. But God was with him [10] and rescued him from all his troubles. He gave Joseph wisdom and enabled him to gain the goodwill of Pharaoh king of Egypt. So Pharaoh made him ruler over Egypt and all his palace.

[11] "Then a famine struck all Egypt and Canaan, bringing great suffering, and our ancestors could not find food. [12] When Jacob heard that there was grain in Egypt, he sent our forefathers on their first visit. [13] On their second visit, Joseph told his brothers who he was, and Pharaoh learned about Joseph's family. [14] After this, Joseph sent for his father Jacob and his whole family, seventy-five in all. [15] Then Jacob went down to Egypt, where he and our ancestors died. [16] Their bodies were brought back to Shechem and placed in the tomb that Abraham had bought from the sons of Hamor at Shechem for a certain sum of money.

[17] "As the time drew near for God to fulfill his promise to Abraham, the number of our people in Egypt had greatly increased. [18] Then 'a new king, to whom Joseph meant nothing, came to power in Egypt.'[c] [19] He dealt treacherously with our people and oppressed our ancestors by forcing them to throw out their newborn babies so that they would die.

[20] "At that time Moses was born, and he was no ordinary child.[d] For three months he was cared for by his family. [21] When he was placed outside, Pharaoh's daughter took him and brought him up as her own son. [22] Moses was educated in all the wisdom of the Egyptians and was powerful in speech and action.

[23] "When Moses was forty years old, he decided to visit his own people, the Israelites. [24] He saw one of them being mistreated by an Egyptian, so he went to his defense and avenged him by killing the Egyptian.[25] Moses thought that his own people would realize that God was using him to rescue them, but they did not. [26] The next day Moses came upon two Israelites who were fighting. He tried to reconcile them by saying, 'Men, you are brothers; why do you want to hurt each other?'

[27] "But the man who was mistreating the other pushed Moses aside and said, 'Who made you ruler and judge over us? [28] Are you thinking of killing me as you killed the Egyptian yesterday?'[e] [29] When Moses heard this, he fled to Midian, where he settled as a foreigner and had two sons.

[30] "After forty years had passed, an angel appeared to Moses in the flames of a burning bush in the desert near Mount Sinai. [31] When he saw this, he was amazed at the sight. As he went over to get a closer look, he heard the Lord say: [32] 'I am the God of your fathers, the God of Abraham, Isaac and Jacob.'[f] Moses trembled with fear and did not dare to look.

[33] "Then the Lord said to him, 'Take off your sandals, for the place where you are standing is holy ground. [34] I have indeed seen the oppression of my people in Egypt. I have heard their groaning and have come down to set them free. Now come, I will send you back to Egypt.'[g]

[35] "This is the same Moses they had rejected with the words, 'Who made you ruler and judge?' He was sent to be their ruler and deliverer by God himself, through the angel who appeared to him in the bush. [36] He led them out of Egypt and performed wonders and signs in Egypt, at the Red Sea and for forty years in the wilderness.

[37] "This is the Moses who told the Israelites, 'God will raise up for you a prophet like me from your own people.'[h] [38] He was in the assembly in the wilderness, with the angel who spoke to him on Mount Sinai, and with our ancestors; and he received living words to pass on to us.

[39] "But our ancestors refused to obey him. Instead, they rejected him and in their hearts turned back to Egypt. [40] They told Aaron, 'Make us gods who will go before us. As for this fellow Moses who led us out of Egypt—we don't know what has happened to him!'[i] [41] That was the time they made an idol in the form of a calf. They brought sacrifices to it and reveled in what their own hands had made. [42] But God turned away from them and gave them over to the worship of the sun, moon and stars.This agrees with what is written in the book of the prophets:

"'Did you bring me sacrifices and offerings
forty years in the wilderness, people of Israel?

[43] You have taken up the tabernacle of Molek
and the star of your god Rephan,
the idols you made to worship.
Therefore I will send you into exile'[j] beyond Babylon.

⁴⁴ "Our ancestors had the tabernacle of the covenant law with them in the wilderness. It had been made as God directed Moses, according to the pattern he had seen. ⁴⁵ After receiving the tabernacle, our ancestors under Joshua brought it with them when they took the land from the nations God drove out before them. It remained in the land until the time of David, ⁴⁶ who enjoyed God's favor and asked that he might provide a dwelling place for the God of Jacob.[k] ⁴⁷ But it was Solomon who built a house for him.

⁴⁸ "However, the Most High does not live in houses made by human hands. As the prophet says:

⁴⁹ "'Heaven is my throne,
and the earth is my footstool.
What kind of house will you build for me?
says the Lord.
Or where will my resting place be?

⁵⁰ Has not my hand made all these things?'[l]

⁵¹ "You stiff-necked people! Your hearts and ears are still uncircumcised. You are just like your ancestors: You always resist the Holy Spirit! ⁵² Was there ever a prophet your ancestors did not persecute? They even killed those who predicted the coming of the Righteous One. And now you have betrayed and murdered him— ⁵³ you who have received the law that was given through angels but have not obeyed it."

The Stoning of Stephen

⁵⁴ When the members of the Sanhedrin heard this, they were furious and gnashed their teeth at him. ⁵⁵ But Stephen, full of the Holy Spirit, looked up to heaven and saw the glory of God, and Jesus standing at the right hand of God. ⁵⁶ "Look," he said, "I see heaven open and the Son of Man standing at the right hand of God."

⁵⁷ At this they covered their ears and, yelling at the top of their voices, they all rushed at him, ⁵⁸ dragged him out of the city and began to stone him. Meanwhile, the witnesses laid their coats at the feet of a young man named Saul.

⁵⁹ While they were stoning him, Stephen prayed, "Lord Jesus, receive my spirit." ⁶⁰ Then he fell on his knees and cried out, "Lord, do not hold this sin against them." When he had said this, he fell asleep.

In Acts 13:13-43 the apostle Paul and companions also similarly reviewed Jewish biblical history in Antioch of Pisidia.

Here is some more Jewish future in the coming of the New Jerusalem down from Heaven. Revelation 7 lists the 12 tribes of Israel as sealed by the living God. This is written about again in Chapter 14 about the same 12 tribes in heaven who have Jesus name and His Fathers name written on their foreheads. Revelations 21:12 tells of the Holy City, Jerusalem, coming down out of Heaven from God. It has 12 gates and the names of the 12 tribes of Israel are on the Gates.

In verse 14 on the 12 walls foundations of the city are the names of the 12 Apostles of the Lamb.

Again, we will have plenty of time to meet and talk with all of them!

CHAPTER 6

Uniting the Church Militant for the Final Battle

Christ is the head of the body, the Church (Colossians 1:18). The church has the power, command, and purpose, to bring Him back. Therefore go and make disciples of all nations, baptizing them in the name of the Father and of the Son and of the Holy Spirit and teaching them to obey everything I have commanded you and surely I am with you always, to the end of the age – or "the completing of the line of the graph".

As you look forward to the day of God and speed its coming! II Peter 3:12. Now there is in store a crown of righteousness to all who have longed for His appearing. II Timothy 4:8. Always give yourselves fully to the work of the Lord because you know that your labor in the lord is not in vain. II Corinthians 15:58.

1 Corinthians 1:7 New International Version (NIV)

[7] Therefore you do not lack any spiritual gift as you eagerly wait for our Lord Jesus Christ to be revealed.

Philippians 3:20 New International Version (NIV)

[20] But our citizenship is in heaven. And we eagerly await a Savior from there, the Lord Jesus Christ,

Hebrews 9:28 New International Version (NIV)

[28] so Christ was sacrificed once to take away the sins of many; and he will appear a second time, not to bear sin, but to bring salvation to those who are waiting for him.

Hebrews 10:25 New International Version (NIV)

[25] not giving up meeting together, as some are in the habit of doing, but encouraging one another—and all the more as you see the Day (on the graph) approaching.

This chapter is written to all "who look for His appearing" and is a plea to all the churches to unite and pressure "the line" to completion!

- ❖ Perhaps a synod or some uniting body could be created and empowered by all denominations to complete the line. God loves variety in His children so there are many different assemblies of Christians. We are still all one body because we all belong to His family. We must continue outreach in our communities and throughout the world but now join with one purpose to translate the Scripture and reach every tongue, tribe and nation:

Revelation 7:9 – After this I looked and there before me was a great multitude that no one could count, from every nation, tribe, people, and language standing before the Throne and in front of the Lamb. I thought of this huge number one day as I was cleaning sweet corn. Each kernel had a "string" leading to it from the top which could represent a connection to one person, or to people or to a whole church. There are many seeds on one cob and each one could produce another cob with many seeds. So, one seed could multiply into millions in time. The first "kernels" could have been Adam and Eve, the Old Testament saints as Abraham, Isaac and Jacob up to our time now. We must now be planting or sowing the seed of the Word to help produce the huge number in our Father's house.

Matthew 24:14 says "and this gospel of the Kingdom will be preached in the whole world as a testimony to all nations, and <u>then the end will come.</u>

<u>When I saw the graph from Wycliiff Translators, it appeared to me that this is the most defining answer from Jesus as to when He will return to take us to the place He has prepared.</u> All God's children, look to and live for this and He gives us power to bring Him back. Let us join forces and resources in obedience to the Great Commission.

Following is a January 2018 progress report from Wycliffe, one of several translators. Because of your faithful partnership Wycliffe Associates is currently working on projects in over 76 countries worldwide. These projects include:

Empowering national Bible translators
Providing technology and training in support of Bible translation
Building Bible translation training centers
Digital publishing
….and much more

Vision 2025 in action:

3,703 New Testament translations in progress
2,758 Translations yet to begin
346 New translation project starts in 2017

Please note the projection of a book of the Bible, maybe like the Gospel of John, in every language by 2025. That is in only 5 years! Technological advances enable this process but once a translation occurs the work to disseminate the life giving Word takes time. The power of the Holy Spirit and the prayers of His people will facilitate this work. Many living today may be alive when He returns. That is why you see so many young people on fire for Jesus today. I Thessalonians 4:16d-17 "and the dead in Christ will rise first. [17] After that, we who are still alive."

So, "let the church arise", as a recent song implores. There are many different "types" of Christian churches that now should lay aside differences and unite to "hasten the day". This involves Catholicism, Baptist, Reformed, Evangelical, Anglican, Lutheran, Presbyterian, Methodist, Anabaptist, Pentecostal, Nondenominational, Amish, Mennonite, Independents, and all others who long to see Him. In addition to these churches are many organizations that are committed to spreading the Word. Here is a list as examples of them. They include, Jews for Jesus, Wycliffe, Christian Reformed World Missions, Thru the Bible Broadcast, Mission India, World Net

Daily, American Bible Society, Gospel to the World ministries, World Gospel Mission (WGM), World Gospel Outreach (WGO), International (AMG) English Language Institute (ELIC) World Vision, International, plus many more.

On searching, I have found a list of translators throughout the world. Wycliffe works in partnership with them.

Association Centrafricaine pour la Traduction de la Bible et l'Alphabetsation (ACATBA)
Assoc Linguistica Evangelica Missionaria (ALEM)
Bible Translation Association (BTA)
Bible Translation and Literacy (BTL)
Indian Institute for Cross Cultural Communications (IICCC)
Nigeria Bible Translation Trust (NBTT)
Translation Association of the Philippines (TAP)
Vanuatu Christian Council, Vanuatu Bible Translation (VCC-VBT)
Evangel Bible Translators (EBT)
Global Bible Translators (GBT)
Institute for Bible Translation (IBT)
International Bible Society (IBS)
The Lockman Foundation
Lutheran Bible Translators
Pioneer Bible Translators
United Bible Societies
World Bible Translation Center (WBTC)
Wycliffe Bible Translators

Recently I have received a letter from Resonate Global Mission with the following message. "The work of missionaries, church planters, campus pastors, and ministry leaders have grown the global church in amazing ways, but the work isn't finished. More than 1.5 billion people still have not heard the Gospel." This task is too great for independent work so we must unite to "finish the task". We need to combine our resources, effort, and pray to the Lord of the Harvest. As we work and pray we will be able to see the line on the graph move in response – a visible answer to work and prayer.

Now comes the predicted, difficult times as we work. As Satan sees the progress of the church militant he must try to stop the progress and ultimately the line on the graph. Christians are being killed in increasing numbers. Muslims are responsible for most of this persecution. Satan is trying to spread them throughout the world as refugees to other countries to aid in stopping the propagation of the Gospel and promoting evil. But we can tell these people about Jesus and by the power of the Spirit they will gain eternal life. Violence is spreading to all countries because of him. He even kills his own, possibly to keep them from finding Jesus. As the Muslim population moves due to terrorism or whomever they use, we must show them the Way. They are descendants of Abraham through Ishmael and God loves them and has many that must turn to Him.

Again, at this time in history, we are experiencing increasing violence throughout the world. Refugees are fleeing many oppressive governments, and many lose their lives in the process. Religious persecution, murder, and other "end times" predictions are growing in number also, in the United States. We are blessed with a large amount of resources and Christians that use them for spreading the good news. A raging spiritual battle is occurring that many ascribe to politics. Satan knows if the United States was destroyed, it would take longer to spread the Gospel. Our economic, military, freedom, and spiritual power is for that purpose. We must be in constant prayer for those He put in power in our government.

As we get closer to the end of the age we must be ready to suffer for Jesus and His word sake. We must unite to hasten the day and not be deterred because of that threat.

The one major concept that separates us is the Adiaphora. Paul in Colossians 2:16 says, "therefore do not let anyone judge you by what you eat or drink or with regard to a religious festival, a new celebration or a sabbath day. In Titus 3:9 he says "But avoid foolish controversies and genealogies and arguments and quarrels about the law because these are unprofitable and useless. In addition, I would recommend reading all of Romans 14. The first three verses introduce this chapter which thoroughly covers these possible hindrances to work together.

Colossians 2:16 and Titus 3:9 refer to these religious practices in which we differ to a certain extent. This would be like what we eat or drink, what day to gather – Saturday or Sundays, baptism modes, regulations, and other differences. We must be conscious of what and how we practice as someone has said "When traditions are drained of purpose they become rituals." It is knowing and loving Jesus and the Father's sacrifice that only matters. And of course, His teaching to love one another, how to live, and tell the world about salvation through Christ alone. So one must not let religious practices keep us from being one church, with one God, with one purpose to unite and hasten the day. In Luke 4:43 Jesus said He must spread the good news, and that is why He was sent! We must certainly do this because <u>we are sent for this!</u>

I am not saying to get rid of our differences, as God likes variety in His children. We may baptize babies or adults by sprinkling water or immersion. We may celebrate the Lord's Supper in various ways or times. Profession of faith may be any age (Joel 2:28-29 as a reminder). You may eat anything you want if it does not offend anyone of faith. We may worship and fellowship together on any day we regard as holy. God looks at our heart as we do things to please Him. He delights in that like any human parent. Hebrews 10:25 instructs us by saying "Let us not give up meeting together as some are in the habit of doing but let us (we who join together to bring Him back) encourage one another and <u>all the more as you see the Day approaching.</u>

So, it is not works that unites us. It is our all-powerful Savior. In John 17:3 when He prays for Himself, His disciples and us He said, "now this is eternal life: that they may know you, Father, the only true God and Jesus Christ whom you have sent". This Jesus unites us.

Think of the church this way. In a choir, band, or orchestra you have a variety of voices and instruments, and the ability to sing or to play the instruments. Up front is a conductor and all eyes are on that person. We are the ones singing or playing and the conductor is the Holy Spirit. He directs and manages us who have a wide variety of talents and gifts. Together we fulfill the wishes and commands of the Holy Spirit and make fine music.

Then there is the music; soprano, tenor, alto and bass. It takes the gifts of the Holy Spirit to have ability to perform. Romans 12:6 We have different gifts, according to the grace given to each of us. If your gift is prophesying, then prophesy in accordance with your[a] faith. These gifts are clarified further in 1 Corinthians 7:7, 1 Corinthians 12, 1 Corinthians 14:12, I Timothy 4:14, II Timothy 1:6-7, Hebrews 2:4 and I Peter 4:10.

Now there is the music to play for the audience. We must sing and play the beautiful music of Scripture to the lost world. John 3:16 is the title of the song written by our God. We must share our faith, preach, teach, proclaim, live out our love for God in front of others, love others, help those in spiritual, mental and physical distress. We must give financially to kingdoms work and be in constant prayer for healing and for others salvation. Let us be faithful in producing this music. Witnessing could be a soprano or praying could be tenor or a sharing your faith could be an alto or and giving or sharing could be a bass.

Our Conductor gives us the ability to read the music – the Word of God. I Corinthians 12 Paul reviews the spiritual gifts (our abilities to sing and make music). And in verse 11 he says "all these are the work of one and the same Spirit, and He gives them to each one, just as He determines. He also tells us in Romans 12:4-5. "Just as each of us has one body, with many members and those members do not all have the same function, so in Christ, we who are many form one body and each member belongs to all the others." <u>Let us now form that one body and together produce the music that will move the line and bring Jesus back!</u>

One more important chorus is the children's choir. Mission India has Bible classes for children in India and have wonderful stories of how they lead their families to Christ. Churches in the area of south Grand Rapids, Michigan, support Streams of Hope, which serves the community by helping families in need and having spiritual advisors. Many children attend their Bible classes and other such pursuits in building their faith that could be the only contact with Scripture for many.

When you visit flower gardens, either of your own or in stores, the beauty and makeup or their design appears fascinating. When there are many in a small area (or even one plant) they may appear "loud" in their countenance. That is because they comprise a chorus with many sounds from soprano to bass, or of a variety of musical instruments making music of praise to their creator.

The prophet Joel says God will pour out His spirit on your sons and daughter. Psalm 8:2 says "from the lips of children and infants you have ordained praise. In Matthew 18:5 Jesus said "And whoever welcomes one such child in my name welcomes me." So teaching little children about Jesus will help bring Him back.

Now referring back to the numbers give by Wycliffe in Vision 2025 where they report 3,771 translations yet to begin should motivate God's people to unite and speed this process. Possibly with united effort of the churches, and of course in the Power of the Holy Spirit, we could change the vision to year 2022! It will take some time for those receiving the translated Bible, even like just the Gospel of John, to come to know and accept Jesus in their heart. The Holy Spirit will, if we ask Him, to speed the acceptance up. Very soon after the work is done, He will return.

At the time of this writing Rev Billy Graham went home. He mirrored the person of John the Baptist who prepared the way of the Lords first coming to earth. Rev. Graham has faithfully ministered the word of God throughout the world including to many of the nations leaders. His theme was always John 3:16. He did not change or compromise the Biblical message that Jesus is the only way to the Father and salvation is in Him alone, (John 17:3). The Holy Spirit surely spoke through him in preparing the Way. Dr. Graham preached to millions of people throughout the world and did not elevate himself but only Jesus Christ.

His funeral was even a powerful testimony and witness. His body was in the US capital Building Rotunda for several days and displayed a cross of flowers. The messages and prayers given were a sermon to many who heard. John the Baptist prepared the way for Jesus first coming. (Matthew 3:1-3). Reverend Graham has now prepared the way for Jesus second coming. Could he be John the Baptist II?

Here is one more incentive to unite us and bring the good news to everyone. Romans 10:14-15 says "How then can they call on the one they have not believed in? And how can they believe in the one whom they have not heard? And how can they hear without someone preaching to them?" In Matthew 5:14a and 16b Jesus says "you are the light of the world – let your light shine before men, that they may see your good deeds and praise your father in heaven." I Peter 3:15 says "Always be prepared to give an answer to everyone who asks you to give the reason for the hope you have.

Therefore, since we are surrounded by such a great cloud of witnesses, let us throw off everything that hinders and the sin that so easily entangles. And let us run with perseverance the race marked out for us, ²fixing our eyes on Jesus, the pioneer and perfecter of faith. For the joy set before him he endured the cross, scorning its shame, and sat down at the right hand of the throne of God. ³Consider him who endured such opposition from sinners, so that you will not grow weary and lose heart. (Hebrews 12:1-3)

In Matthew 13 Jesus tells the Parable of the Sower. We, His people, are the sower of the seed of the Word given to us by the Holy Spirit. We must witness to everyone that we can or are led to all types of soil, and the Holy Spirit opens the hearts to receive Jesus. We must promote the work of sowing with love of neighbors and prayer. In many cases one sows and another reaps. You may only meet someone once or several times who sees Jesus living in you and hears your testimony or witness. Someone else may be the reaper who further works in the person's spiritual life. Maybe a missionary, neighbor, minister or you. Sower and reaper may be glad together as one sows and another reaps. (John 4:36c-37)

Jesus worked to "bring salvation to those who are waiting for Him" (Hebrews 9-28d). As effective sowers and reapers "you ought to live holy and godly lives as you look forward to the day of God and speed its coming (2 Peter 3:11-12). We together can speed His coming!

In Psalm 133 God says He is pleased when we live together in Unity. Let us do that now and work together as we now see the time rapidly approaching for the bridegrooms return. Let us be as the 10 wise virgins (Matthew 25:1-13) and be ready. We must also be faithful in telling the 10 foolish virgins to be ready, sharing with them the "sufficient quantity of the oil of the Word." Now, while there is time!

As mentioned several times, one major purpose of this writing is to unite all of God's people and do the final work of missions. Most Christians today, perhaps 95% will answer the question "how soon is Jesus coming back" will answer "soon but probably in 50-100 years". This does make for a complacent attitude and living for which I am also guilty.

Mission work suffers because of this. Many missionaries are underfunded and lack help. If we do not approach this together with understanding, conviction, excitement, enthusiasm, joy, eagerness, a sure hope, and anticipation, most will keep the drag of this attitude of living -"it will be a long time but not in my lifetime". Jesus return will be a complete surprise.

If we missionize together the work will increase one hundred-fold or more. Remember, this is a command of Jesus with no options!! So, let us now work together with the excitement and expectation that comes with working for the Holy Spirit who opens the hearts of those to whom we bring the Good News! When he saw the crowds, he had compassion on them, because they were harassed and helpless, like sheep without a shepherd. ³⁷Then he said to his disciples, "The harvest is plentiful, but the workers are few.³⁸Ask the Lord of the harvest, therefore, to send out workers into his harvest field."(Matthew 9:36-38) What a privilege He gives us and what unimaginable rewards we will receive in Heaven!

Here is an appropriate song for all of us.

Brightly Beams Our Father's Mercy
Text and music: Philip Paul Bliss, 1838–1876

1. Brightly beams our Father's mercy
   From his lighthouse evermore,
   But to us he gives the keeping
   Of the lights along the shore.

2. Dark the night of sin has settled;
   Loud the angry billows roar.
   Eager eyes are watching, longing,
   For the lights along the shore.

3. Trim your feeble lamp, my brother;
   Some poor sailor, tempest-tossed,
   Trying now to make the harbor,
   In the darkness may be lost.

CHORUS: Let the lower lights be burning;

Send a gleam across the wave.
Some poor fainting, struggling seaman
You may rescue, you may save.

In conclusion, three events must occur before Jesus Christ, our precious Savior returns.

1. The fulness of the Jews, His chosen people.
2. The fulness of the Gentiles also His people.
3. The word of God, the Scriptures or the revelation of Jesus Christ, Savior of the world, who says "And this gospel of the kingdom will be preached in the whole world as a testimony to all nations, and then the end will come."

The Holy Spirit has chosen the body of Christ, the church, to do this work. What a blessing as He could do it without us! We are commanded to make Him known to all peoples and cannot do it alone or as individual churches or denominations. We must unite in the Spirit with the reward of having a part in His return.

In John 17:23 Jesus is praying for us and says to our Father "I in them and you in me. <u>May they be brought to complete unity to let the world know that you sent me</u> and have loved them even as you have loved me".

CHAPTER 7

Love

"because God is Love" 1 John 4:8

Who is God and what is He like?

The One and only true God is the Yahweh or Jehovah who created the world, its people, and everything in the entire universe. None can begin to "understand" His being. He is so much greater than any creature, people or angel, and He is beyond comprehension. He is infinite. We can know Him by the Word He has given us with understanding by the power of the Holy Spirit. In Isaiah He says in Chapter 44:8 "you are my witnesses. Is there any God besides me? No, there is no other Rock, I know not one". You see, He searched all of space and beyond (too vast for anyone to grasp) and did not find any other God. He has no beginning and no end. He is eternal. In Isaiah 44:6 "I am the first and the last, apart from me there is no God." In Isaiah 43:10 God says "Before me no God was formed, nor will there be after me. In Isaiah 43:11 and 45:5 He says "I, even I am the Lord and apart from me there is no Savior. In Isaiah 46:9 He says, "I am God and there is no other and there is none like me."

God tells us of the oneness of His being as many false religions have many gods because of Satan's teaching. They espouse power over man having an ego that must be satisfied at man's expense. There is no love there, only hatred and darkness. The one true God, whom we love and serve, has no ego to satisfy. (He even washed His disciples' feet! John 13:5) Regarding this He says in Philippians 2:5-11 "your attitude should be the same that Christ Jesus had. Though he was God, he did not demand and cling to his rights as God. He made himself nothing, (Christmas Day Celebration for us)he took the humble position of a slave and appeared in human form. And in human form he obediently humbled himself even further by dying a criminal's death on a cross. Because of this, God raised him up to the heights of heaven and gave him a name that is above every name, so that at the name of Jesus every knee will bow in heaven and on earth and under the earth, and every tongue will confess that Jesus Christ is Lord, to the glory of God the Father." Again regarding pride God says in Matthew 20:24-28 "when the ten heard about this, they were indignant with the two brothers. Jesus called them together and said, "You know that the rulers of the Gentiles lord it over them, and their high officials exercise authority over them. Not so with you. Instead, whoever wants to become great among you must be your servant, and whoever wants to be first must be your slave just as the Son of Man did not come to be served, but to serve, and to give his life as a ransom for many." He is infinite and over all with no question about this fact. To worship Him is a "natural occurrence" as He has created everything. It is not learned or acquired but innate in every human being. We are made in His image.

The commands of our heavenly Father is not to show His power or authority over us, that is a given, but He knows what is best for His children and He loves us the infinite amount as much as He is infinite. He knows what we should and should not do. He knows what would harm us. If you see your little child near the edge of a cliff, you would tell him to get back immediately. This is not to show parental authority but to keep your child safe from danger. It is important to think of God as your Father for that is how He reveals Himself. So now, when you talk with Him you go to our intercessor, Jesus Christ, any time or place you find yourself. There is no special place or physical position that you must be in. With Jesus, we go right into His presence! Our earthly parents were made in His image and we could go to them anytime any place with any request. They love us and we love them. This typifies or is a picture of our relationship to our Heavenly Father. You may talk with God while driving, waking up in the night, walking, reading Scripture, in meetings, at church, on a tour, in any circumstance you may find yourself. What an amazing, loving God is ours! Psalm 62:8 says "Trust in Him at all times, Pour out your hearts to Him for God is our refuge". He is like a loving parent. We are made in His image-likeness or similar traits – somewhat like a child inherits a nature from his parents. So, when you see a little child with arms around the parent's neck holding tightly as he/she is carried, this is a picture of God carrying us or holding our hand while walking. He is the strong parent who so loves us and we are the little child holding on for dear life. This is why parents must love their children and carry them so they will envision their relationship to their Heavenly Father when they are adults. In Psalm 103:13 God says "as a father loves or has compassion on his children, so the Lord has love and compassion on those who love him." Isaiah 40:11 describes our God and says "He tends His flock as a shepherd, He gathers the lambs (that is all of us) in His arms and carries us close to His heart."

Recently, in a Christian Book store I witnessed some parents pushing their little boy in a wheelchair. It appeared he had a bodily disorder of uncontrollable, involuntary motions that limited his ability to function properly in life. Looking at the parents I thought of our Father. In spite of their sons' limitations they loved him. That was their little boy and he belonged to them. He was theirs no matter what his condition. This is what it is like with our God who loves in spite of our weakness, brokenness, and extreme limitations, especially in our spiritual lives. In Psalm 103:14 He says, "I know how you are formed, I remember that you are dust." In spite of this Jesus says in John 17:23 "that you Father sent me and have loved them even as you have loved me." In other words, God loves His children as much as He loves Himself! 1 John 3:1 "How great is the love the Father has lavished us, that we should be called the children of God! And that is what we are!"

In Deuteronomy 10:12-20 God tells Israel and us again who He is. "And now, O Israel, what does the Lord your God ask of you but to fear the Lord your God, to walk in all his ways, to love him, to serve the Lord your God with all your heart and with all your soul, and to observe the Lord's commands and decrees that I am giving you today for your own good?"

To the Lord your God belong the heavens, even the highest heavens, the earth and everything in it. Yet the Lord set his affection on you and loved and chose you. For the Lord your God is God of gods and Lord of lords, and great God, mighty and awesome, who shows no partiality and accepts no bribes. Fear the Lord your God and serve him. Hold fast to him and take your oaths in his name. He is your praise; he is your God.

Love the Lord your God and keep his requirements, his decrees, his laws and his commands, always.

What I see God saying here is this, He wants love and obedience from you His children. It is the same with you and your children (we are made in His image). But, He wants you to love Him first and most of all, then obey Him because you love Him. The theme of the Word of God is love. This is the meaning too of the Lords Supper and Baptism.

The false gods of this world want obedience but not love because Satan cannot love.

So talk with Him often and tell Him you love Him, not by commandment any more, but because you are His child. He longs for this from you.

Say, "Father, we all confess our love for you and ask your Holy Spirit to empower us to live for you and that others may see you living in our hearts. Show yourself to the world through us so others may come to know and love you too."

Think of this. Because He is our Father, do the earth, sun, moon, galaxies, and all He has created belong to us as we are His sons and daughters?

His love is infinite with no bounds or limit. That is why loving, serving, and worshipping Him is not a religion. It is a relationship! Why would one not want to love and serve Him and instead worship a false god? The one true God then is best described by the word LOVE. This is a universal word existing in heaven and earth and all of infinite space. I could not find an adequate definition. Its immensity defies complete understanding because our God is infinite and cannot be defined and understood by anyone but Himself. Listen to what He says in Psalm 103:11-12. "For as high as the heavens are above the earth, so great is His love for those who love Him. As far as the east is from the west so far has He removed our transgressions from us!" These scripture texts summarize the Old Testament. The New Testament explains how He fulfilled His promises and removed our sins.

John 3:16

[16] For God so loved the world that he gave his one and only Son, that whoever believes in him shall not perish but have eternal life.

This text is the summary of all Scripture as the old axion "The New is in the Old contained, the Old is by the New explained is made clear. Love is what God wants most from us. He wants obedience because that is best for us. If we love Him we will do that. Here is what Jesus says is the first and greatest commandment as found in Matthew 22:37-40.

[37] Jesus replied: "'Love the Lord your God with all your heart and with all your soul and with all your mind.'[a] [38] This is the first and greatest commandment. [39] And the second is like it: 'Love your neighbor as yourself.'[b] [40] All the Law and the Prophets hang on these two commandments."

Jesus also gave this commandment in Deuteronomy 6:5. Please note this especially if you are Jewish.

When we go to Jesus for comfort, healing, or share our joy, we go to the One who not only knows all things because He is God, but is the One who is like us in the flesh except for sin. He knows exactly how you feel or what you are experiencing. He lived all the emotion and negative effects of sin on the human body. He knows your grief, your joy, and your physical pain because He had this too. So, bring everything from joy to hurts, to the One who knows and rejoices or hurts with you. John 4:6-"Jacob's well was there, and Jesus, tired as He was from the journey, sat down by the well. It was Almost noon" He emptied Himself of His Godly existence in Heaven left His Father who is now our Father, to become human like us to save us. "For we do not have a high priest who is unable to empathize with our weaknesses, but we have one who has been tempted in every way just as we are – yet he did not sin". Hebrews 4:15-16. What a Savior!

In Mark 11:11 Jesus goes into the Temple and looks around. I picture this as no one else is there and He is alone. I can imagine Him looking at all the decorations, the structure, the altars and other objects there. He can see Himself in them all. They all pointed to Him and his sacrifice. What a sad and sorrowful feeling He must have experienced as it pointed to the pain and suffering He would soon endure. He did not back out then as I would have done. His love for us kept Him steadfast. His Father and the Holy Spirt were there with Him but the thought of them forsaking Him is an indescribable, horrible feeling. So you can see that Jesus was human and suffered like mankind. Hebrews 2:14 says, "since the children have flesh and blood, Jesus too shared in their humanity so that by His death He might destroy him who holds the power of death"-the devil…In verse 18 God says, "Because He himself suffered when He was tempted, He is able to help those who are being tempted."

The Old Testament contained many laws that pointed to Jesus and were designed to keep His people from the false gods worshipped by the nations around them. They had idols and rituals that made them feel they had a god to worship. All peoples that are born have an innate knowledge of one who created all things and must be worshipped. So, the rituals helped the pagans express this innate knowledge and desire to worship a god. But the people of the one true God, once you know and love Him, this love, by the Holy Spirit is no longer by commandment but is a natural occurrence somewhat like the love between a man and his wife, a faint likeness of our loving God. The love between a man and woman is not by a commandment but comes "naturally" for His people.

If you are reading this and do not know Jesus, I plead with you to call on Him to give you life. Here is what He says in Ezekiel 18:32. "For I take no pleasure in the death of anyone", declares the Sovereign Lord. Repent and live! This is what our God is like. He wants you to come and love Him. Again, in Ezekiel 33:11 Jesus says, "I take no pleasure in the death of the wicked, but rather that they turn from their ways and live!" He is pleading with you and the purpose of this book is to have people turn to Him.

In a parable in John 14 a wayward son takes his inheritance, leaves his father and loses it all in riotous living. When he returns home, his father <u>runs to meet him</u> to take him back. His father celebrates his return. This is a picture of our loving heavenly Father as He rejoices when wayward children return to Him. How can you not love Him?

The older brother was not happy that his father rejoiced over his "bad brother". We must be delighted to see others come to know Jesus no matter what their past because our Father is!

He says in Luke 15:10, "There is rejoicing in the presence of the angels of God over one sinner who repents."

When Jesus was dying on the cross He asked His Father (our Father now John 17:21) to forgive those who were torturing and killing Him. He was forgiving the people there and us. It was our sins that put Him there. The love that God the Father, Jesus, and the Holy Spirit has for us is seen in Jesus sacrifice on the cross. The infinite pain that our Triune God suffered, the separation, and forsaking Himself (Jesus), as He suffered physical pain too. This shows how great and incomprehensible and infinite His love for us is. Are you able to comprehend such love and that of our Father and the Holy Spirit?! Would you not want to serve this one only true God rather than the myriads of false gods dreamt up by man inspired by the evil one? This one true God loves you with an infinite love that everyone longs for. Universally since time began everyone wants to be loved because that is who He is. We are made in His image and therefore want to be loved. Fulfill then this longing which is in every heart and love Him. No other love will satisfy as seen and experienced in the secular world. I am appealing, God is appealing you to come and worship Him!

In John 17:3 where Jesus is talking to our Father and to us says "Now <u>this is eternal life:</u> that they may <u>know you,</u> the <u>only true God,</u> and <u>Jesus Christ,</u> whom <u>you have sent.</u>"

On searching a Bible Concordance for the words, love, lover, lovely, loving, loving kindness, beloved and loved, I found these words were used approximately 875 times in the entire NIV Scriptures. These words expressing passion, feeling and affection are important to God for He is love. Being in His image makes this the most sought after and desired strong passionate feeling by all peoples. That is what is portrayed in the movies, weddings, stories, books and the like. However, true love is only found in the children of God.

Following are some "love texts" from Scriptures to read.

Genesis 20:13	Ecclesiastes 9:1
Exodus 34:6	Song of Solomon 1:2, 8:7
Leviticus 19:18	Isaiah 55:3
Numbers 1:18	Jeremiah 31:3
Deuteronomy 5:10, 7:9, 11:1	Lamentations 3:22
Joshua 22:5	Ezekiel 16:8
Judges 5:31	Daniel 9:4
2nd Samuel 7:15	Hosea 3:23
I Kings 10:9	Joel 2:13
2 Chronicles 9:8	Amos 5:15
Ezra 3:11	Jonah 4:2
Nehemiah 9:17	Micah 6:8
Esther 4:15-16	Zephaniah 3:17
Job 37:13	Zechariah 4:2
Psalm 32:10, 33:5, 33:18, 115:1, 145:8, 147:11	Malachi 4:2
Proverbs 3:3	

From the New Testament

Matthew 12:18	II Thessalonians 3:5
Mark 12:30-31	I Timothy 6:11
Luke 10:27	II Timothy 1:13
John 13:34, 14:15-17	Titus 3:4
Acts 2:45	Philemon 1:5
Romans 5:8	Hebrews 10:24
I Corinthians 13:1-3, 2:9	James 1:12
II Corinthians 13:11	I Peter 1:8
Galatians 5:22	II Peter 1:17
Ephesians 2:4-5, 3:18-19	I John 3:1
Philippians 2:2	II John 1:6
Colossians 3:14	III John 1:21
I Thessalonians 4:9	Revelation 2:19

The names of the Triune God helps us also to understand who He is. Here are some names of God found in the Scripture that He gave to help us know and love Him.

Adonai – My Great Lord
El – The strong One
El Elohe Yisrael – The God of Israel
El Elyon – The God Most High
Elohin – The all Powerful One
El Olam – The eternal God
El Roi – The God who sees me
El Shaddai – The all sufficient one
Immanuel – God with us, the I am
Jehovah – I am the One who is
Jehovah- Jireh – The Lord will provide

Jehovah – Mekaddishkem – The Lord who Satisfies
Jehovah Nissi – The Lord is my Banner
Jehovah-Rapha – The Lord who heals
Jehovah – Rohi The Lord my Shepard
Jehovah -Sabboth – The Lord of Hands
Jehovah Shalom – The Lord is Peace
Jehovah – Shammah – The Lord my companion
Jehovah – Tsidkenu- The Lord our Righteousness
Yah, or Jah- I am
Yhwh – I am – the one who is

Some names of Jesus:

Almighty
Author and Finisher
Beloved
Bromch
Bread of Life
Bridegroom
Bright Morning Star
Carpenter
Chosen One
Chief Cornerstone
Door
Emmanuel/Immanuel
Eternal Father
Faithful and True Witness
Firstborn
God
Head of the Church
Holy One
Hope
I Am
Image of the Invisible God
Jesus
Judge/Ruler
King of Kings

Lamb of God
Last Adam
Light of the World
Lion of the Tribe of Judah
Living Water
Lord of Lords
Man of Sorrows
Master
Messenger of the Covenant
Messiah
Prince of Peace
Prophet
Redeemer
Resurrection and the Life
Savior
Shepard
Shiloh
Son of God
True Vine
The Way, The Truth and the Life
Wisdom of God
Wonderful Counselor
Word
Yahweh (Jehovah)

In Colossians I the Holy Spirit describes our Jesus who is very God of very God.

The Supremacy of the Son of God

[15] The Son is the image of the invisible God, the firstborn over all creation. [16] For in him all things were created: things in heaven and on earth, visible and invisible, whether thrones or powers or rulers or authorities; all things have been created by him and for him. [17] He is before all things, and in him all things hold together. [18] And he is the head of the body, the church; he is the beginning and the firstborn from among the dead, so that in everything he might have the supremacy. [19] For God was pleased to have all his fullness dwell in him, [20] and through him to reconcile to himself all things, whether things on earth or things in heaven, by making peace through his blood, shed on the cross.

Names of God the Holy Spirit:

Breath of the Almighty	Spirit of God
Counselors	Spirit of Yahweh
Comforter	Spirit of Grace
Spirit of Counsel	Spirit of Knowledge
Eternal Spirit	Spirit of Truth
Free Spirit	Spirit of Understanding
God	Spirit of Wisdom
Good Spirit	Spirit of Life
Holy Spirit	Spirit of the living God
Lord	Spirit of prophecy
Power of the Highest	Spirit of Revelation
Spirit of Might	Spirit of the Father
Spirit of Adoption	Spirit of the fear of the Lord
Spirit of Burning	Spirit of the Lord
Spirit of Judgement	Spirit of the Son
Spirit of Jesus Christ	Spirit
Spirit of Glory	

After the trumpet call, gathering of His people, crowning of Jesus, singing songs like the "Messiah", we will celebrate.

The Wedding Feast of the Lamb

The Apostle Paul in I Thessalonians 4:13-18, by revelation of the Holy Spirit, describes what will happen when Jesus returns. As you can see He will call your name and take you to Heaven. John 14:2-4. There will be row upon row of tables with bread and wine by each setting. Jesus will call you by name and after you see His side, hands and feet with the wounds, you will give Him a loving hug (your heart will fill up with perfect, overwhelming love when you see Him) and then He will show you your place at the table. (John 17:24). The first celebration we will do when everyone is together is the Wedding Feast of the Lamb promised in Revelation 19:6-8. Here one will experience the infinite love of God for us without the barrier of sin that hinders us. Jesus spoke of this feast in Matthew 26:29 when He instituted the Lords Supper, sometimes called the last supper. Jesus said to His disciples "I tell you, I will not drink of this fruit of the vine from now until I drink it anew with you in my Fathers Kingdom." <u>The celebration now of the bride-the church, and the bridegroom-Jesus, will be the First Supper!</u> Then the angel said to me: "Write this : Blessed are those who are invited to the wedding supper of the Lamb!" Revelation 19:9. There will be people from every tribe, tongue, and nation (Revelation 5:9). Mary, Jesus mother will be sitting by Him. At the table your loved ones will sit close by you. Also, your brothers and sisters in Christ that you met here on earth. Those that accepted Jesus because you shared your faith with them will be thanking you. Ministers missionaries, and those whom the Holy Spirit used to bring the good news of Jesus will be very busy accepting the gratitude of those they taught. It is a good thing that we will have eternity to welcome everyone. That is only one part, of course, for God has so much for us.

We will need the time to thank those who taught us and those who witnessed to our ancestors. Someone took my Grandmother to Sunday School in the Netherlands, beginning the faith journey that was a blessing to many that followed her. I know of many called by God for a life of service. They will be surrounded by thankful hearts as they gather at the feast.

One example is Margaret Njuguna who lives in Nairobi, Kenya where she serves at the En-Gedi Children's Home. By faith, Margaret started this home in 2014. En-Gedi serves children with disabilities, many of whom have never been shown love or given any rehabilitation. Some of those children who can't walk or talk or very disabled are discarded by their parents. At this writing she has 12 children and shows them God's love by caring for them. So amazing! In heaven, who do you think will be surrounding her?

Now that we will all be together the prayer of Jesus in John 17:20-26 is fulfilled.

[20] "My prayer is not for my disciples alone. I pray also for those who will believe in me through their message, [21] that all of them may be one, Father, just as you are in me and I am in you. May they also be in us so that the world may believe that you have sent me. [22] I have given them the glory that you gave me, that they may be one as we are one— [23] I in them and you in me—so that they may be brought to complete unity. Then the world will know that you sent me and have loved them even as you have loved me.

[24] "Father, I want those you have given me to be with me where I am, and to see my glory, the glory you have given me because you loved me before the creation of the world. Now one can understand that when we see Jesus we will see our Father and our Holy Spirit though they are invisible. Anyone who has seen me has seen the Father (John 14:9)

[25] "Righteous Father, though the world does not know you, I know you, and they know that you have sent me. [26] I have made you[a] known to them, and will continue to make you known in order that the love you have for me may be in them and that I myself may be in them."

As we wait for Him, churches, lets unite and hasten the day! Let us be encouraged by what the Scriptures say.

Hebrews 9:28 - [28] so Christ was sacrificed once to take away the sins of many; and he will appear a second time, not to bear sin, but to bring salvation to those who are waiting for him.

Hebrews 10:25 - [25] not giving up meeting together, as some are in the habit of doing, but encouraging one another—and all the more as you see the Day approaching.

In John 4:36 – Jesus says "Even now the reaper draws his wages, even now he harvests the crop for eternal life, <u>so that the sower and the reaper may be glad together.</u>"

The 3rd stanzas of the hymn "It is well with my Soul" says "<u>and Lord haste the day when my faith shall be sight</u> the clouds be rolled back as a scroll, the trump shall resound and the Lord shall descend even so it is well with my soul."

Psalm 27:4 New International Version (NIV)
[4] One thing I ask from the LORD,
    this only do I seek:
that I may dwell in the house of the LORD
    all the days of my life,
to gaze on the beauty of the LORD
    and to seek him in his temple.

We can hasten the day!!

Here is a time line from AD1 to AD33 – 33 years that changed History dramatically.

From: Jesus Birth in Luke 2:7
    And Mary gave birth to her first-born son

To: His death in Luke 23:46
    Jesus cried out with a loud voice "It is finished!"

To: His resurrection in Luke 24:6
    He is not here, He is risen

To: His ascension in Luke 24:51
    While he was blessing them, He left them and was taken up into Heaven.

To: His return, promised in Acts 1:11

"Men of Galilee the angel said, "why do you stand here looking into the sky?" This same Jesus who has been taken from you into Heaven, will come back in the same way you have seen Him go into Heaven." (Maybe around 2025?) In Revelation 22:7 He says "Look, I am coming soon! Blessed is the one who keeps the words of the prophecy written in this scroll." And in Revelation 22:20 He who testifies to these things says, "Yes, I am coming soon." Amen. Come, Lord Jesus.

We are able to make it soon if we work together for Vision 2025!

Here is a choice we have as an incentive to work hard to move the line to completion. I Thessalonians 4:16-17 says "and the dead in Christ will rise first. After that we who are still alive will be caught up in the clouds to meet the Lord in the air." Death has lost its power over us but it still hurts to lose a loved one. Now if we fervently work together to bring Him back, many who are alive today will not see death nor suffer the pain of losing a loved one!

AND ON WHAT DAY WILL JESUS RETURN? I BELIEVE IT WILL BE ON EASTER OR ASCENSION DAY !!!!!

Epilogue

At the time of this writing there is an increase in violence and unrest and killing of Christians is more numerous. Family members are killing family members as love is going cold. Destructive violent storms and earthquakes are becoming common. It almost appears more evident that Satan is being let loose and is trying to stop the line on the graph. He is trying to stop the process and progress as we in obedience carry out the eleventh commandment – the Great Commission. As the time for completion nears there will be more persecution of God's people, more intimidation, harmful actions, extreme murders, suicides, threats and love that goes cold. All a part of the sign of the times in which we live. We must be warned that as we work it will become more difficult as Satan tries to step in. We, our children and grandchildren, must be spiritually strong to endure.

This should motivate us to action! I feel that this is an emergency. We must unite to get the Word out to every corner of the world. Time is not on our side and since the last presidential election many are becoming more hostile to Christianity, but God is using freedom and prosperity to do His work. That is why we have such extraordinary blessings. The United States is the only power in this world that can keep order to allow us to do the work of evangelism. Thankfully there are people who often pray over the president (Vice President Pence is a born-again Christian), as he and his family are attacked every day, clearly by those who hate God. This is unprecedented. This is not politics but a raging spiritual battle!

Because of Jesus soon return, I urge you, from now on, look at History as it affects and effects the spreading of the word of God. Pray for peace so the gospel may go throughout the world. Hopefully God will use the United States to make a world environment that enables us to work. Do not look at events as political, or that's life, or that's the way it is, but how do they help or hinder the work.

For instance, the dictator of North Korea who threatened the United States with nuclear missiles just met with the leader of South Korea, crossing the DMZ for the first time. He also has an upcoming meeting with the President of the United States. Could these two first time meetings be a way to peace in that area? Most importantly will this then allow the Gospel to go into North Korea where people are starving for spiritual and physical food. Or, as time passes, is Satan going to make peace efforts fail and cause the specter of nuclear war to stop the spread of the Word and persecute the Christians in China and the Korea's? What about President Trump pulling out of the nuclear treaty with Iran? He judges it as a deceitful unworkable deal. Iran is threatening severe consequences. Will new peace talks bring harmony and amity in the area so the gospel may go through the Mid-East, especially for Israel? Or will this be the beginning of what Jesus said in Matthew 24:15-21 that Israel will be destroyed and to flee the city? The nations that surround Israel want to destroy her but it will not happen until just before Jesus return. He said "For then, there will be great distress, unequaled from the beginning of the world until now – never to be equaled again. If these days had not been cut short, no one would survive." Note that the plagues described in Revelation 16 resemble the effects of nuclear war and radiation that causes sores, blood in seas, scorching sun, pain, earthquakes and much more. Some of these horrific events were experienced in Hiroshima and Nagasaki, Japan. Never before in history were such weapons that could end life on earth.

Will the economy of the United States improve, which will help finance the work of missions and enable peace in the world, or will the increasing unprecedented attacks by political and social media on our present elected officials destroy our country's ability to prosper and help keep peace to enable spread of the gospel?

Please, from now on, carefully examine all church and world events in the light of Satan's efforts to slow down the progress of the line on the front cover of this book.

So, now all churches and members that confess that Jesus is God and long for His promised appearing must unite with one goal, that is to "hasten the day". Laying aside the adiaphora and differences and combining resources and efforts to bring Him back! Let us use the Power that Jesus sent in Acts 1:8. "But you will receive power when the Holy Spirit comes on you; and you will be my witnesses in Jerusalem, and in all Judea and Samaria, and to the ends of the earth!

In I Corinthians 12, Paul discusses the church, the bride of Jesus, as the human body. The hands, feet, arms, legs, tongue, eyes, ears and nose are all needed for one to live and function. None is above the other and if one part hurts the whole body suffers. Let us unite as one body equipped for one purpose and press on together what we are offered and commanded to do.

Make the work of mission be your passion. Love your neighbor as yourself. Be concerned about them knowing Christ Jesus. Be faithful and aggressive in sharing your faith, and as others "read your life" (II Corinthians 3:3). as you live it may you sing the song "May the beauty of Jesus be seen in me". Be a faithful witness for Christ. There are so many neighbors that do not know Him. Share your faith in your conversation with others letting them see the hope you have and offer that to them. In the neighborhood of the church I attend there is reported 56% without a church home. Though the presence of churches and the visible symbol of the cross is a testimony to non-believers they must be told in love, the way to eternal life. There is a quote that says "you may be the only Bible that someone reads."

Verse #2 of the hymn "The Church's One Foundation" says:

Elect from every nation yet one o'er all the earth, Her charter of salvation, one Lord, one faith, one birth: One holy name she blesses. Partakes one holy food and to one goal she presses, with every grace endued.

Verse #3 speaks of the tribulation and the longing eyes of the church that is finally victorious and at rest.

Verse #3 of It is well with my soul says "and Lord haste the day when my faith shall be sight, the clouds be rolled back as a scroll, the trump shall resound, and the Lord shall descend, even so, it is well with my soul."

Then verse #2 of "They'll know we are Christians by our love" describes us as we work. "We will walk with each other, we will walk hand in hand and together we will spread the news that God is in our land." 1 Peter 3:15 always be prepared to give an answer to everyone who asks you to give the reason for the hope that you have.

Jesus prayed for such a time as this – the time to unite! In John 17:23 He said to our Father "I in them and you in me. May they be brought to complete unity to let the world know that you sent me and have loved them even as you have loved me."

As a summary of this writings purpose, God, through the apostle Paul, says in 2 Corinthians 5:20 "We are therefore Christ's ambassadors, as though God were making His appeal through us." One definition of ambassadors is "a representative of the highest rank sent by one government or ruler to other." So let us unite and tell the world of Jesus and that of His soon return!

Let us be faithful in giving to those organizations that bring the Gospel throughout the world. Pray for and communicate with those in foreign countries as some report that there are persecuted Christians that feel abandoned by God's people. Make comments of encouragement with your donations to be passed on to our distant brothers and sisters in Christ.

There is little excitement among God's people today on this subject as it was about three or four decades ago. In conversation today when you say Jesus is coming soon the response is flat and the idea is given that it will be a while and not in our lifetime. This suppresses enthusiasm for showing this truth and living in this sure hope. The apostle Paul spoke often of this expectation and was energized by it even though it was 2000 years ago.

However, the evidence is convincing and exciting. Never before in the history of the Word or the world did the surety of <u>WHEN</u> existed. Together we the church of Christ are able to complete the work Jesus gave us, and with passion, excitement, prayer, and with the Holy Spirit can bring Him back!

Jesus told us exactly what must occur before He returns. Never before did the church have:

- Spiritual understanding
- Worldwide presence
- Numbers
- Freedom
- Finances
- Ease of life in freedom
- Technology
- Instruments
- Printing press and paper
- Worldwide communication devices
- Translation ability
- Needed transportation
- Education

Can we create an organization that will concentrate and emphasize Jesus soon return? Maybe call it "Homecoming"? This will accelerate all mission supports and activity. We will focus on telling the world of Jesus and the sure hope we have. Finally, <u>one truth that unites us all</u> and the real reason what the work of the church militant is. Ministering on end times will motivate us and result in witnessing, sharing the Good News, rather than seeking only our own spiritual growth every Sunday. Let us live now as if He is coming back in five (5) years and make it a reality!

So we must pray, finance, and work with each other toward one purpose, and one goal.

"God loves you because of who God is, not because of anything you did or didn't do."

1 Corinthians 2:9 New International Version (NIV)

[9] However, as it is written:

"No eye has seen, no ear has heard, and no human mind has conceived"[a] the things God has prepared for those who love him—

Psalm 27:4 Make this your passion! "One thing I ask of the Lord, this is what I seek: that I may dwell in the house of the Lord all the days of my life, to gaze upon the beauty of the Lord and to seek Him in His temple."

In conclusion these three occurrences must take place before Jesus Christ returns as promised. The church is commanded to do this being appointed by the Holy Spirit.

1. The fulness of the Jews
2. The fulness of the Gentiles
3. "And this gospel of the kingdom will be preached in the whole world as a testimony to all nations, and then the end will come." Matthew 24:13

PRESENT DAY ALERT

The present Covid 19 pandemic has made Jesus return appear closer than my first contemplation. Maybe we do not have 5 more years per vision 2025. This world wide pandemic could be an early forerunner to motivate and prepare us for the final battle. The lockdown and troubling atmosphere is causing a spiritual revival as many are appealing to our God for help and comfort. Comfort from the Word and with singing of spiritual songs via all forms of media is unprecedented and uplifting.

So, today's disturbing events could be a taste of what the final happenings will be or could this be the beginning of the actual beginning. One could envision the present situation as end times described by Jesus. He said those times will be terrible, as none before, and intolerable for any life on earth. Maybe this could be motivation for God's people to complete 2025!

How can we know if this is just a precursor or if it is the onset? As mentioned in Chapter 3 the United States of America has been blessed economically to complete gospel spread and military power to keep order in the world to enable completion of the line on the graph and Vision 2025. So, with all the internal discord (not a political but in reality, a spiritual battle) and if the economy goes into a great depression, I believe the end times events will commence.

Do not be afraid. God has prepared a place for us and will then soon return to call us up by name. Heaven is a place of love, joy, peace, pleasure and real life. What will be the most wonderful, beautiful, indescribable joy for us? We will meet Jesus in whom is the infinite love of God.

VISION 2025

By the year 2025 a Bible IN EVERY LANGUAGE!
Wycliffe Associates

And this gospel of the kingdom will be preached in the whole world as a testimony to all nations and then the end will come.

Matthew 24:14

Septuagint

Some 200 years before Christ 70 scholars in Egypt translated the Old Testament from Hebrew to Greek. This translation became known as the Septuagint.

Targums

Long before Jesus was born, oral translations of scripture, called Targums, were being made in Jewish synagogues. A translator would stand beside the reader and translate the passages into the local Aramaic language. As early as 100 BC there were written Aramaic versions of the Old Testament, although most of the written versions appeared after the time of Christ.

Vulgate

In the fourth century Jerome revised an earlier Latin version of the Bible. His version, called the Vulgate, was for many centuries the only version authorized by the Roman Catholic Church. It was, therefore, the Bible of the Christian world.

| 200 | 100 | 0 | 100 | 200 | 300 | 400 | 500 | 600 | 700 | 800 |

PHOTO: George Cowan translating Scripture with Mazatec co-translator in Mexico, circa 1950.

Who have the translations been for?

Prior to 1800

The majority of Bible translators prior to 1800 were bilingual Christians who translated from another language into their own mother tongue. Jerome, for example, translated into Latin, Wycliffe into English and Luther into German. They translated for established churches which had heard the gospel long before and had been existing on foreign language Scriptures.

After 1800

Around 1800 European Protestants began to take the Good News around the world. Their mission fields were generally colonies governed by their respective countries. The Englishman William Carey, for instance, went to the British colony of India.

Increasingly, Bible translators after 1800 were missionaries who translated into languages they learned in order to preach the gospel. They used their translation for evangelism, teaching, church planting and church growth. The Bible Society movement, with its burden for Scripture distribution, coincided with this era.

After 1950

By the middle of the twentieth century, the colonial era was coming to an end. A strong worldwide movement for political independence brought many new independent nations into being. Increasingly, many of these nations are requiring that their own people take over tasks previously done by foreigners.

Today there is a need for both kinds of Bible translators—those who translate into their mother tongue and those who translate into an acquired language.

Our members continue to pioneer—learning languages in order to translate, as well as encouraging others to develop the skills and vision for Bible translation. Where there are mother tongue speakers with a vision to translate, we train them in vital linguistic and translation skills and provide consultant help. We provide similar help for speakers of national languages, such as Spanish or French, who are translating for a minority group.

Who's done the translations?

Prior to 1450

During the Middle Ages there was little vision for Scriptures in a person's mother tongue. The Roman Catholic church insisted on the use of Jerome's Latin version. It discouraged the use of Scriptures by anyone except clergy, scholars and kings, on the grounds that the unlearned would misinterpret it. Few people, even among the clergy, lawyers and kings, could read. Handwritten copies of the Bible were

Bible Translation Through the Ages

by George Cowan with Carol Schatz

1982 1763

Number of languages with at least one complete book of Scripture.

Around 1450
Renaissance;
Reformation;
Gutenberg's press

Around 1800
Beginning of
Protestant missions;
Bible translation as
tool in evangelism.

523

Wycliffe's Bible

John Wycliffe, an Oxford scholar, completed the first English translation of the Bible in the 1380s.

Luther's Bible

Martin Luther, German reformer, completed his translation of the Bible into German in 1534.

KJV Bible

The King James Version was published in 1611. It was translated by 54 scholars under orders from King James of England.

1934
Wycliffe Bible Translators and the Summer Institute of Linguistics training and field work began. (The organizations were formed in 1942.)

33

67

| 1000 | 1100 | 1200 | 1300 | 1400 | 1500 | 1600 | 1700 | 1800 | 1900 | 2000 |

---

extremely expensive. The few translations that were produced were in the dominant languages of the ancient world, such as Latin and Coptic, and in early European languages.

After 1450

Around 1450 the climate for Bible translation changed. The Renaissance brought a new emphasis on learning, so that even the common man was encouraged to learn to read. The Reformation stressed the importance of knowing Scripture. Gutenberg's invention of a printing press with moveable type brought the price of a Bible within the reach of ordinary people. As a result of all this, there was new interest in the translation of the Bible into the major languages of Europe.

1933–1934

The year 1933 was a landmark year for Bible translation. Spiritual and secular developments came together to make it the beginning of the modern Bible translation movement for ethnic people groups.

1) In Keswick, New Jersey, L.L. Legters reported to the Keswick conference on a trip to South America. The Lord sent an unusual burden on

the conferees to pray for unreached tribes.
2) In Keswick, England, John Savage of Peru also challenged conferees to pray for the unreached tribes. Again the Lord sent an unusual burden.
3) In the scientific world, Leonard Bloomfield published his book, **Language**, which provided a basis for describing and writing previously unwritten languages.

God had given W.C. Townsend a tremendous vision for the Bible in every person's language. It was time to act on that vision. In 1934, Townsend and L.L. Legters

began the Summer Institute of Linguistics (also known as Camp Wycliffe) to train young people in linguistics so they could translate the Bible into all of the world's languages. Wycliffe Bible Translators was organized in 1942. Eugene Nida later promoted these linguistic principles in Bible Society circles.

Since 1934

Since 1934 pioneer translation efforts have majored on non-European languages. Literacy campaigns have been carried on simultaneously with translation efforts.

The Bible Societies have increasingly worked with

national believers to revise existing Scriptures and to produce "common language" versions.

Wycliffe Bible Translators and the Summer Institute of Linguistics have focused on providing Scripture for people who have never had a translation in their language. This includes (1) language groups where there are churches but no Scriptures and (2) groups where there are no churches and there is little or no understanding of the gospel. In most cases, their languages have never been written.

President Reagan has proclaimed 1983 "The Year of the Bible." While making the proclamation, he said, "Inside (the Bible's) pages lie all the answers to all the problems man has ever known."

A deep conviction of the importance of the Bible's message is what has motivated Bible translators throughout the ages. Committed to making that message clear at any cost, Bible translators have given years, and sometimes their very lives, to see the task completed.

That task was begun some 200 years before Christ, when 70 scholars in Egypt translated the Hebrew Scriptures into Greek. It is still going on. In fact, the vision has never burned as brightly as it burns now. Before 1900, 523 language groups received their first piece of translated Scripture. Between 1900 and 1982 the figure was 1,240.

During the course of history Bible portions have been translated and published in 1,763 languages. More specifically:

279 language groups have had a complete Bible.

551 language groups have had a complete Testament but not a whole Bible.

933 language groups have had at least one complete book but not a whole New Testament.

_____
1,763 Total*

*Figures courtesy of the American Bible Society

NOTE: Some 300 of these translations are no longer in use, either because they are unavailable or because the languages are no longer spoken. The rest of them are still providing God's answers to men's problems

Targums

Long before Jesus was born, oral translations of scripture, called Targums, were being made in Jewish synagogues. A translator would stand beside the reader and translate the passages into the local Aramaic language. As early as 100 BC there were written Aramaic versions of the Old Testament, although most of the written versions appeared after the time of Christ.

Vulgate

In the fourth century Jerome revised an earlier Latin version of the Bible. His version, called the Vulgate, was for many centuries the only version authorized by the Roman Catholic Church. It was, therefore, the Bible of the Christian world.

Septuagint

Some 200 years before Christ 70 scholars in Egypt translated the Old Testament from Hebrew to Greek. This translation became known as the Septuagint.

| 200 | 100 | 0 | 100 | 200 | 300 | 400 | 500 | 600 | 700 | 800 |

PHOTO: George Cowan translating Scripture with Mazatec co-translator in Mexico, circa 1950.

Who have the translations been for?

Prior to 1800

The majority of Bible translators prior to 1800 were bilingual Christians who translated from another language into their own mother tongue. Jerome, for example, translated into Latin, Wycliffe into English and Luther into German. They translated for established churches which had heard the gospel long before and had been existing on foreign language Scriptures.

After 1800

Around 1800 European Protestants began to take the Good News around the world. Their mission fields were generally colonies governed by their respective countries. The Englishman William Carey, for instance, went to the British colony of India.

Increasingly, Bible translators after 1800 were missionaries who translated into languages they learned in order to preach the gospel. They used their translation for evangelism, teaching, church planting and church growth. The Bible Society movement, with its burden for Scripture distribution, coincided with this era.

After 1950

By the middle of the twentieth century, the colonial era was coming to an end. A strong worldwide movement for political independence brought many new independent nations into being. Increasingly, many of these nations are requiring that their own people take over tasks previously done by foreigners.

Today there is a need for both kinds of Bible translators—those who translate into their mother tongue and those who translate into an acquired language.

Our members continue to pioneer—learning languages in order to translate, as well as encouraging others to develop the skills and vision for Bible translation. Where there are mother tongue speakers with a vision to translate, we train them in vital linguistic and translation skills and provide consultant help. We provide similar help for speakers of national languages, such as Spanish or French, who are translating for a minority group.

Who's done the translations?

Prior to 1450

During the Middle Ages there was little vision for Scriptures in a person's mother tongue. The Roman Catholic church insisted on the use of Jerome's Latin version. It discouraged the use of Scriptures by anyone except clergy, scholars and kings, on the grounds that the unlearned would misinterpret it. Few people, even among the clergy, lawyers and kings, could read. Handwritten copies of the Bible were

Original 1983 Inspirational Graph From

Bible Translation Through the Ages

by George Cowan with Carol Schatz

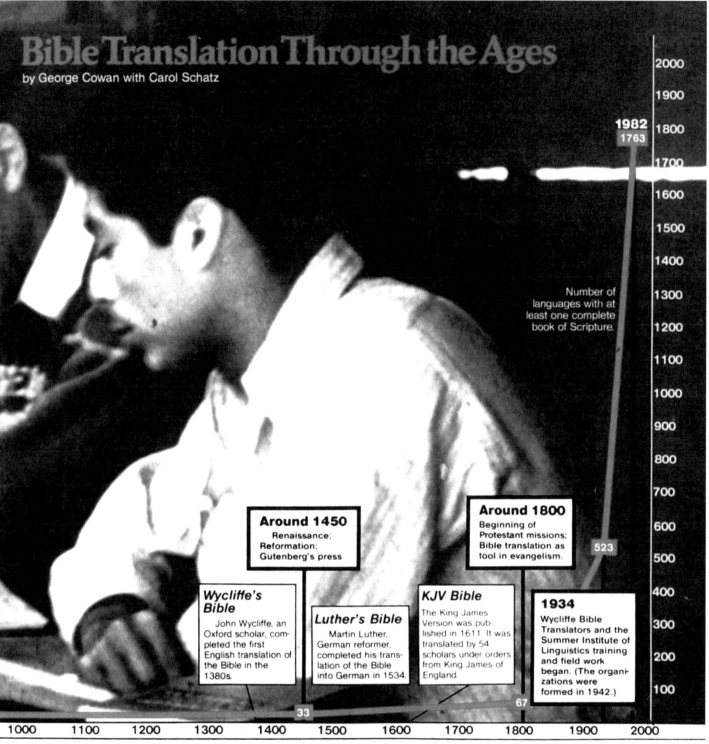

2000
1900
1800

1982
1763

1700
1600
1500
1400
1300

Number of languages with at least one complete book of Scripture.

1200
1100
1000
900
800
700

Around 1450
Renaissance; Reformation; Gutenberg's press

Around 1800
Beginning of Protestant missions; Bible translation as tool in evangelism.

600

523

500

Wycliffe's Bible

John Wycliffe, an Oxford scholar, completed the first English translation of the Bible in the 1380s.

Luther's Bible

Martin Luther, German reformer, completed his translation of the Bible into German in 1534.

KJV Bible

The King James Version was published in 1611. It was translated by 54 scholars under orders from King James of England.

1934
Wycliffe Bible Translators and the Summer Institute of Linguistics training and field work began. (The organizations were formed in 1942.)

400
300
200
100

33

67

| 1000 | 1100 | 1200 | 1300 | 1400 | 1500 | 1600 | 1700 | 1800 | 1900 | 2000 |

---

extremely expensive. The few translations that were produced were in the dominant languages of the ancient world, such as Latin and Coptic, and in early European languages.

After 1450

Around 1450 the climate for Bible translation changed. The Renaissance brought a new emphasis on learning, so that even the common man was encouraged to learn to read. The Reformation stressed the importance of knowing Scripture. Gutenberg's invention of a printing press with moveable type brought the price of a Bible

within the reach of ordinary people. As a result of all this, there was new interest in the translation of the Bible into the major languages of Europe.

1933—1934

The year 1933 was a landmark year for Bible translation. Spiritual and secular developments came together to make it the beginning of the modern Bible translation movement for ethnic people groups.

1) In Keswick, New Jersey, L.L. Legters reported to the Keswick conference on a trip to South America. The Lord sent an unusual burden on

the conferees to pray for unreached tribes.
2) In Keswick, England, John Savage of Peru also challenged conferees to pray for the unreached tribes. Again the Lord sent an unusual burden.
3) In the scientific world, Leonard Bloomfield published his book, **Language**, which provided a basis for describing and writing previously unwritten languages.

God had given W.C. Townsend a tremendous vision for the Bible in every person's language. It was time to act on that vision. In 1934, Townsend and L.L. Legters

began the Summer Institute of Linguistics (also known as Camp Wycliffe) to train young people in linguistics so they could translate the Bible into all of the world's languages. Wycliffe Bible Translators was organized in 1942. Eugene Nida later promoted these linguistic principles in Bible Society circles.

Since 1934

Since 1934 pioneer translation efforts have majored on non-European languages. Literacy campaigns have been carried on simultaneously with translation efforts.

The Bible Societies have increasingly worked with

national believers to revise existing Scriptures and to produce "common language" versions.

Wycliffe Bible Translators and the Summer Institute of Linguistics have focused on providing Scripture for people who have never had a translation in their language. This includes (1) language groups where there are churches but no Scriptures and (2) groups where there are no churches and there is little or no understanding of the gospel. In most cases, their languages have never been written.

Wycliffe Bible Translators

19

Printed in the United States
By Bookmasters